ATROPOS PRESS
new york • dresden

THANK YOU
FOR BEING PART
OF THE MASTERCLASS
PROTOTYPE !
WITH NEW FRIENDSHIP.

© by Nicoletta Iacobacci
Think Media EGS Series is supported by the European Graduate School

ATROPOS PRESS
New York • Dresden

151 First Avenue # 14, New York, N.Y. 10003

978-1-940813-39-4

EXPONENTIAL ETHICS

by Nicoletta Iacobacci

TABLE OF CONTENTS

7

TO NICHOLAS

Learn from yesterday, live for today,

hope for tomorrow.

The important thing is not to stop questioning.

—*Albert Einstein*

ACKNOWLEDGMENTS

This work would not have been possible without the support of the Rockefeller Foundation Bellagio Center, which hosted me for a residency. There, I was able to finish the draft of this book. A warm and sincere thank you to Pilar Palacia, director of the Bellagio Center, for believing in both me and my work.

This book is the result of a Ph.D. thesis that ended, to my astonishment, with a summa cum laude. Therefore, I would like to express my sincere gratitude to my advisor and friend, professor Wolfgang Schirmacher, founder and, at that time, program director of the European Graduate School. He has guided and supported me since the day I began attending classes at EGS. He's a tough, but very sympathetic advisor and one of the smartest and most knowledgeable people I know. He encouraged my research and allowed me to become a "thinker."

When I decided to apply to EGS, I was at a turning point in my life. Successful in my career, although unchallenged and unmotivated, I decided to start a new chapter and go back to school. I was looking for an unusual academic institution. When I found EGS, I knew it was a steep path to acceptance given my basic philosophical experience, but I wanted to try. Wolfgang encouraged me, saying that philosophy is not only an academic subject but also a journey—one that, if I was "contaminated," I would never abandon.

Hence, I resigned from my job at the European Broadcasting Union to embark on this new, lengthy adventure. I know I will continue this journey, not as a pure philosopher since I started too late, but as a contributor to a new ethical framework addressing the exponential growth of technology. To trigger global actions on new moral principles, we need to facilitate global public conversation among several disciplines, both humanistic and scientific. Based on my experience and network, I could easily be one of the architects of this feat.

My list of thanks and acknowledgements is long, but I'd like to start with EGS professors who made my Ph.D. experience productive and stimulating: Giorgio Agamben, Michael Hardt, Alain Badiou, Simon Critchley, Diane Davis, Chris Kraus, Mitchell Joachim, Manuel De Landa, Sylvère Lotringer, Lev Manovich, Avital Ronell, Volker Schlöndorff, Judith Balso, Victor Vitanza, Slavoj Zizek, and Frederick Kittler, who gave us his last lectures before his end.

I want to thank Ellen Zheng Yue for supporting the Chinese version of this book and AiMin Peng for the Chinese translation.

I am very grateful to Natascia, who every day of this journey has inspired me, given me energy and useful advice, encouraged me, and acted as a sparring partner—always motivating me to continue, to never give up.

I'd like to thank Antonella for her consistent medical advice and for dissolving some of the doubts I had during my journey, and Adam who was initially involved in reviewing my text.

I must also acknowledge Silvia, Katharina, Ferhan, Sara, Ariane, Derrick, and my editor Crystal, who saw my work growing and followed me in the making of my Ph.D. thesis and in the subsequent book task.

I will also forever be thankful to all my good friends for providing the support and friendship that I needed (too many to list here, but you know who you are!).

This project could not have been completed without the insights and knowledge I acquired attending Singularity University, where I had the opportunity to learn how exponential technologies could address and solve humanity's grand challenges. I also would like to acknowledge, sincerely, TED, and Bruno Giussani for giving me the ability to bridge the gap between my normality and the world's most inspiring and exceptional thinkers. A sincere thank you to

Juan Enriquez, whose "Will our kids be a different species?" TEDTalk ignited the fire in me that started this research.

Lastly, I would like to thank my parents and all of my family for their never-ending support, and most of all, I would like to acknowledge with gratitude my encouraging son Nicholas. His faithful support during the final stages of this book gave me the decisive boost to cross one of the most complex finish lines of my life. Thank you, Nik—*this book is yours!*

FOREWORD

BY JUAN ENRIQUEZ

For four billion years, what lives and dies on this planet has been guided by two laws of nature: Natural Selection. Random Mutation. Then came humans. And they altered the rules. As a result there is now a parallel evolutionary system-logic working alongside that of nature. This system's logic is based on Un-natural Selection and Non-Random Mutation.

When humans choose what we eat, what should grow in our gardens, the animals we will tolerate, or not tolerate, they are determining what they want to live and die. A park left fallow would quickly look far, far different that Central Park Hyde Park, or the Tuileries. A farm untended would not grow fields of wheat or rows of corn. A small Chihuahua left to wander the African plain would soon be selected out. We now determine, shape, breed about half of what lives and dies on the planet.

And in the past few decades we have developed instruments to fundamentally alter the gene code of the organisms we like or dislike. The mutations we introduce into corn to make it drought tolerant or pesticide tolerant are non-natural. The way we engineer bacteria to produce our foods and medicines is non-natural. The way some of us alter our bodies to grow taller or prevent certain diseases is non-natural.

While we introduced some unwanted creations into nature, and fundamentally altered ecosystems, this paralleled evolutionary track we created generates enormous benefits. Billions are able to eat enough, get cured, or prevent a host of formerly deadly diseases. Our overall lifespan and increasing quality of life is extraordinary.

But with great power, power to determine what lives and dies, comes great responsibility. We are increasingly able to redesign life forms to suit our purposes. We are increasingly in charge of evolution—including the evolution of our own species. This terrifies many.

But historically, there have been dozens of proto-humans on the planet. We lived side by side and even bred with some of them. It is normal and natural for variants of species, and for various related species, to live side by side. What is un-natural, in terms of the history of life on this planet, is for there to be one and only one human species.

Historically it has been quite hard to stop scientific discovery cold. Societies that jettisoned science and research typically crashed and burned. But there are examples where we have regulated, limited, reshaped what we can and cannot do with science. This occurs by broad consensus, not because one dictator or one society decrees it so. We can hide, fear, anguish about our growing power, or we can try to understand it, reshape it, guide it intelligently.

As we understand what we can do with life, we need to marry science, ethics, and society, to understand and make tradeoffs in all we can accomplish. I hope you approach a fast moving, controversial field with an open mind and understand some of the tradeoffs involved. Almost all of us non-vegetarians like the notion of eating free-range, wholly organic meat. But letting goats or cattle loose is one of the most destructive things we can do on a broad scale. All of us would prefer to reduce any risk of harm to our children, but when one chooses to do so by foregoing "un-natural" vaccinations, one unleashes deadly epidemics. All of us would like our medicines to be safer, but too much of an emphasis on safety and too little emphasis on faster-better-cheaper means the cost of new treatments explodes and the time to market expands.

Life is about tradeoffs. There is no one right path or answer. We have certainly mucked up great swaths of the planet. But we also learn. We learn to protect species. To bring back large swaths of European forests. To eat more consciously. To cure more diseases. And perhaps, how to redesign our bodies so that they better adapt to environments very different from Earth.

Natural Selection and Random Mutation will never permanently take us off this planet. Right now things like bone and vision loss damage most astronauts. If we are to ever dream of exploring, of truly reaching out for the stars, of becoming an interplanetary species, we will have to alter some fundamental aspects of ourselves. What is acceptable, what is not, how fast, how far, are all subject to debate. But I hope you are able to think about redesigning life not just with a sense of fear and dread but with a sense of possibility, of wonder, of potential. We need to act carefully, but, as a species that has thrived on change and exploration, we need to act.

Enter Nicoletta's book... As we try to understand where science can take us, what it can do, what it should do, this volume is a good overview of what some scientists are doing, different paths the research may take, what it might mean. You can agree with all of her conclusions, none of them, or, likelier, with a range in between. But you will emerge smarter, better able to understand what is going on, what some of the tradeoffs are, some of the extraordinary possibilities new technology offers.

Juan Enriquez
Managing Director at Excel Venture Management, LLC

INTRODUCTION

The human love affair with technology began with the fashioning of simple tools. In fact, the taming of fire for domestic uses was one of the first—and perhaps most transformative—examples of technological progress. Managing fire was a turning point in human evolution; it provided warmth, heat for cooking, protection from wild animals, and a spot to socialize during the wee hours of the night. Even today people are inclined to gather around campfires, and hosting a fireside chat with experts has become a standard format at most conferences.

Harvard primatologist Richard Wrangham has suggested cooking food was essential to support the rapid development of early hominid brains. He argues that food efficiency is what allowed H. habilis—the "handyman," who started making tools for specific purposes—quickly turned into H. erectus, or "upright man," our first fully standing ancestor. This efficiency allowed our ancestors to chew and digest easily—paving the way for larger brains.

Technology encompasses techniques as simple as language and stone tools to the infinitely more complex artificial intelligence, genetic engineering, and information technology. To our brains, technology is addictive. It enables the releases of dopamine, a neurotransmitter associated with the brain's reward system and plays a critical role in the modulation of our physical movements, memory, attention, emotions, and perceptions of pain and pleasure. Dopamine release, however, can result in dependency. Of course, it is not the technology itself that is addictive, but rather the specific application of choice that triggers the release. This release is part of the love/hate relationship many have with technology. We know such pleasure-seeking behavior can be hazardous, yet we cannot avoid being captivated by it. We're forever driven to find the endless possibilities that exist only if and when we discover them.

On February 11, 2016, scientists around the world celebrated such a discovery, a historical event: physicists at the cutting-edge American lab LIGO (Laser Interferometer Gravitational-Wave Observatory) detected gravitational waves—the ripples in the fabric of space-time proposed by Albert Einstein precisely one hundred years before. Why are gravitational waves significant? They give us a new method to observe space—for example, waves from the Big Bang could help physicists to know more about how the universe formed.

This memorable event symbolized both the dawn of a new astronomy and perhaps the beginning of an era of exponentially growing technologies, a possible world populated by ageless, artificial, biomechanical individuals. A phase where rapid technological progress will help us solve many of humanity's grand challenges—energy, education, water, food, and health—while simultaneously posing new ones—relationships with thinking machines, new forms of bioterrorism created by synthetic biology, or the end of privacy, to name a few.

That exponential growth means we will experience progress at mammoth speed in the twenty-first century. Within a few decades, machine intelligence could surpass human intelligence, leading to technological change never before witnessed in the history of all humankind. Soon, these advances could result in the merging of biological and non-biological intelligence, software-based immortal humans and sentient artificial entities.

This epic change poses several ethical questions. Will a new dimension of "humans" emerge? What about the perceptions of human dignity, morality, and autonomy? Will these perceptions survive in their entirety? If we alter the brain to reach intelligence amplification, are we still human? If we remove the faculty of procreation between man/woman with embryos developed in artificial conditions outside the womb, does it make us inhuman?

Other questions emerge, too. Is reprogenetics the new eugenics? (Reprogenetics is the use of reproductive and genetic technologies to select and genetically modify embryos for the purpose of human enhancement.) We should not forget that eugenics, a set of practices aiming to improve the genetic composition of the human race by selective breeding, was promoted and fostered by governments. Conversely, reprogenetics is currently in the hands of the people. Who will control this technology? Are we going to leave the choice to the parents-to-be, who will be able to select their child's genes? Should we set boundaries for this technique? Are governments ready for this radical shift, or will we have to rely on communities of people developing and using future tech to regulate themselves, presumably in the absence of any updated ethical codes?

Further, governments today are already funding projects for developing autonomous robotic systems programmed with enough intelligence to distinguish right from wrong and eventually evaluate moral consequences. But a significant question remains unanswered: how can robots be capable of moral or ethical reasoning when, at times, their inventors are not?

Contemporary transhumanists reason that NBIC (nanotechnology, biotechnology, information technology, and cognitive science) should improve human and non-human natures. Techno-skeptics and bioconservatives, on the other hand, believe that exponentially growing technologies and practices are causing irreversible disruptions. This leads to concern over whether humanity will experience a positive outcome from our ever-advancing technologies or whether it will become the victim of a future of mechanical humans.

Given all that is potentially possible with advancing technology, here are few of the questions that we need to address:

Can we avoid death? If yes, what will be the effects of immortality on society?

Nanotechnology, artificial body parts, smart drugs, and brain boosters can enhance our physiology beyond current human limits—but should we really pursue this? If yes, why?

What are the consequences of persistent human intervention in evolution, and can we interfere responsibly?

Can humans coexist with machines that will be smarter, faster, and more intelligent than we are?

Can we be totally comfortable with human augmentations? What about the ones who won't be able to enhance themselves, due to ignorance or financial troubles?

Will our future still be a "human future" or a cyborg one? Why should we care?

In search of the answers to those questions and others, this book is about the relationships humans will develop with perfected machines. It is about being present to our evolution and aware that technology is growing exponentially while our ethics are struggling to adapt. As soon as we start to grapple with the moral guidelines for one new technology yet another, newer technology appears.

My primary objective is not to develop a new ethical framework but to inform, to ask questions, to initiate discussions, and mostly, to create awareness about the possible consequences of these new technologies. We don't want to slow down our evolution. We want to befriend technology, not run scared from its developments. More than anything, we want to be confident that our children and their children will inherit an extraordinarily bright future, one in which they can coexist peacefully and collaboratively with thinking machines.

After attending TED conferences and Singularity University, I was empowered with new tools and a coherent vision of the future. A future that, if we are not careful, will be governed by technology and by the small groups who control it.

This book is the result of a Ph.D. thesis that was completed almost three years ago. Therefore, some major concepts, although updated, could appear redundant. It has been interesting, though, to verify how speculations that were posed a few years ago could become not only our present but could easily belong to the past. Throughout the process of putting together this book, I can say that I experienced firsthand the intrinsic meaning of "exponentiality."

With this book, I will show how some of the most critical advances in technology are shaping our world and affecting current events. I will look at past and current technologies and speculate on the role they will play in the future. But mostly, I will raise questions about the consequences these emergent technologies may have. They will allow us to remain young, to be free of disease, to become unfathomably brilliant and boundlessly creative, and to be continuously connected to one another. However, if they are not deeply thought about, profoundly and with caution, they could exhaust our humanity.

If this is our evolutionary destiny, we have the opportunity to choose what we will become. As always, the first step toward change is awareness. The primary goal of this book is to enable a practical curiosity on exponentially growing techs and prompt a much-needed conversation on technology, philosophy, and new ethical standards. A discussion that could facilitate a proactive, "crowdsourced" debate—one that could help shaping the code of ethics for the new millennium.

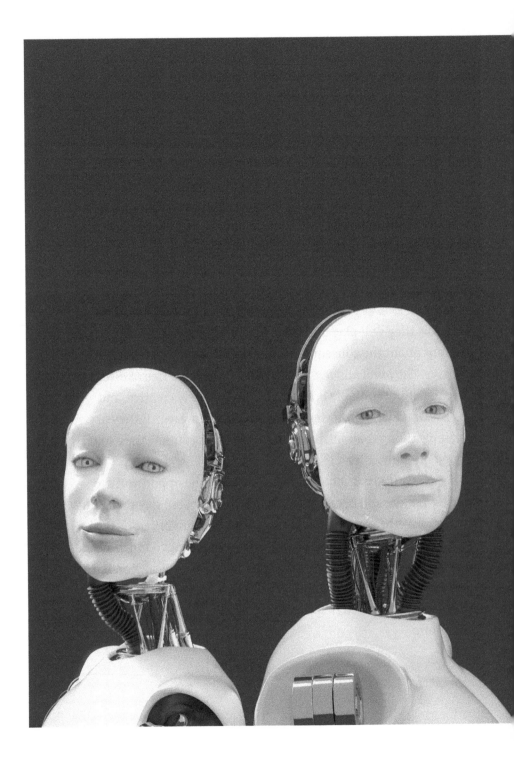

CHAPTER 1:
The coexistence of humankind and machine

EVOLUTION OR REVOLUTION: CAN WE KEEP PACE WITH PROGRESS?

One of the most significant fears we have today is the advance of a super machine that is comparable to or even surpasses the human brain. This begs the question: what happens when man-made machines are produced that are more intelligent than human beings?

What are these man-made machines? Are they robots? Thinking robots?

First of all, what is a robot? At a basic level, a robot is an automated machine programmed to imitate cognitive processes. But there are many different kinds of robots. One kind is *pre-programmed robots* like the ones used to build cars in most automobile plants around the world. These machines need to be previously told what to do, and they operate without changing their activity. They simply execute human instructions. They work alone without human intervention, they seldom make mistakes, they demand only maintenance, and most of the time, they perform better than humans.

Today, we are panicky that the automated workplace will make humans superfluous, but in the long run, we will be fine—at least that's what many experts say. By 2030, as many as 800 million jobs could be lost worldwide due to automation, but the technological advancement itself will create new jobs.

Our history has seen it happen before. In the late-eighteenth century in England, with the First Industrial Revolution—that is, when James Watt's steam engine was applied to textile manufacturing—many jobs disappeared. Before that time, textile production was fulfilled by individual workers in their own premises. When steam power and industrial machinery came along, together with cotton becoming the predominant fabric, laborers started working together in cotton mills, learning new skills, and the textile business was completely disrupted. Even if entire families suffered from this crucial change, it did not lead to major social crisis. As optimists say, technology destroys jobs, but people create new ones.

The foundation for the Second Industrial Revolution came with the arrival of inexpensive electricity applied to mass production. Jobs were lost, but innovations in fields such as steel, oil, and electricity prompted a large number of new jobs. For example, jobs boomed in the transportation sector for railroads, cars, ships, and planes, to name a few. This means workers had to learn new skills, manage new machine tools, and endure in the process of change. And they did, successfully.

The Third Industrial Revolution was even worse for jobs lost due to the use of electronics, transistors, and information technology that automate manufacturing. This revolution was also the dawn of the microprocessor, computers, and telecommunications, which led to the onset of sectors such as space research and biotechnology.

The Fourth Industrial Revolution, however, is not the same as those that came before it. As Klaus Schwab, Founder of the World Economic Forum, warned us, it is unpredictable because it is blurring the lines between the physical, digital, and biological spheres. These synergies are shaping a technological revolution that will be so fast and extreme that not even science fiction is able to fully conceive what our future will be like. Consequently, this rapid growth of technologies doesn't allow us humans to keep up with the transformation, making it increasingly difficult to learn new skills and adapt to this ever-changing framework.

Automation will impact every industry. Almost any job or activity will be affected by robotics, and to protect capacity, there are several aspects to be considered. First, companies should build digital assets and create a more stable and more educated digital force. The latest research by McKinsey and Company indicates that less than 5% of jobs can be entirely automated by current technology since robots can't perform all our tasks. In many cases, then, robots will be an *addition*, not a substitute. Workers, then, need to learn how to operate beside machines or aided by them. Technology can perform repetitive work, therefore freeing up humans to have more exciting occupations. Instead of envisioning a technological Armageddon, workers should be empowered by companies and the overall government to acquire the skills they need to compete in an automated era.

In 2017, the State Council in China released a national strategy for the development of artificial intelligence (AI), aiming to shape the future of AI worldwide. It seems that China wants to delegate social stability to AI, integrating it into a broad range of public services—for instance, in the security, medical, and legal domains. To that end, China has launched a new initiative, an open-source platform. The Chinese government is taking an active role in supporting AI development by positioning itself between startups, which are government supported, and big companies that will remain integral players in the quest of the AI Holy Grail.

China's first wave of open AI platforms will rely on Baidu for autonomous vehicles, Alibaba Cloud for smart cities, and Tencent for intelligent healthcare.

A crucial issue, though, is the overall ethical concerns regarding this open platform and an advanced and rapidly created AI in China, which is often considered to be a country without a moral compass. In the case of AI, however, ethics seems to be something China considered from the start. There is a call for ethics in the state council's document, which set forth that "while vigorously developing artificial intelligence, we must attach great importance to the possible security risks and challenges, strengthen forward-looking prevention and restraint guidance, minimize risks, and ensure the safe, reliable, and controllable development of artificial intelligence."

While AI advances at an exponential pace, robotics is not to be outdone. It seems that affordable personal robots, such as machines that help the elderly or are used in medical environments, may only be 10 years (or less) away.

Apart from pre-programmed machinery, *teleoperated robots* are controlled remotely by a human being. They can be operated by a wire, through a local Wi-Fi system over the Internet, or by satellite. Two primary domains are testing teleoperated robots: the military and the medical domains. The military is using drones for surveillance and for carrying equipment, shooting weapons, and dropping bombs. Whereas, the medical domain, under doctor guidance and across short or long distances, utilizes robots that can perform various tasks, such as surgeries and treatments. Medical robots will soon be able to diagnose patients more precisely—and faster than almost any doctor. But even amid such advancements, we should reflect on the fact that an increasingly de-humanization of medicine is not always a change for the better.

Technology in the medical domain should augment not replace. If we foresee that machines could replace doctors in specific fields, shouldn't we define clear ethical standards? Will we update the "Hippocratic Oath" for a medical robot? What about the physician-patient privilege, the medical confidentiality that is established together with empathy, compassion, and overall, other forms of pro-social behavior?

Further, another class of robots, the *augmenting robots*, can replace the physical capabilities that a person has lost or has never had. Artificial limbs are the most common examples of augmenting robots. Modern prostheses are starting to be connected with the human nervous system. Surgically implanted sensors, for example, pick up signals from the spinal cord and allow people to control mechanized arms by merely envisioning their movement.

3D printing is playing a vital part in the development of augmenting robots. Open Bionics, for example, is a company that is developing affordable and open-source 3D-printed bionic hands for amputees. Enabling the Future, a global network of volunteers, takes a step further. It uses the collective knowledge and passion of a worldwide dedicated community to create a repository of 3D-printed hands and arms, open-source and in the public domain, for those in need of an upper-limb assistive device.

However, human augmentation or human performance enhancement (HPE) could soon be not only medical. In the future, we could be tempted to replace flesh-and-blood limbs with stronger or more fashionable bionic ones and blur the boundaries between the biological and mechanical. Today, we could abhor the idea, or it could even make us laugh—but its eventuality is not so unfeasible.

The more controversial robots are the *autonomous robots* since they are devices that can act and behave with a degree of independence, capable of performing tasks by themselves, without explicit human intervention. Consumer examples range from robot vacuum cleaners to social robots, such as pet robots. Military engineers (mostly in the US, China, and Russia), though, are delving into self-governing war machines. The 9-11 attacks set off an intense development of remote-controlled robots for warfare. Flying drones are becoming common weapons on the world's many battlefields. Military experts and roboticists are envisioning future conflicts undertaken by lethal AI-driven autonomous fighting bots (AI-empowered robots,) genetically modified superhumans, and killer robots. They argue that these self-sufficient machines allow human presence to be in the minority while establishing a safer life-protecting system. It's a morally viable strategy that, by removing soldiers from dangerous and exhausting missions, could diminish civilian and non-combatant casualties.

On the contrary, a 2017 open letter signed by 116 founders of robotics and AI companies urged the United Nations to ban killer robots. The letter stated that *"lethal autonomous weapons threaten to become the third revolution in warfare..."* where weapons without meaningful human control can behave in a dreadful, atrocious way.

Most horrific, what if war-fighting autonomous robots are hacked and become non-autonomous robots controlled by war criminals? Should self-governed machines always be supervised by human control, or can we empower machines with ethical principles?

Robots can be daunting or handy. Scary or empowering. At their core, though, robots are just computer system containers; they are bodies housing sets of coded commands that tell machines what tasks to perform and, eventually, how to behave intelligently. Many robots, however, are not artificially intelligent. Industrial robots, for example, do not require artificial intelligence. They can be programmed to fulfil only repetitive, monotonous tasks.

Conversely, AI-empowered robots have the capability to learn by experience. We can foresee a future where AI will be able to build its own artificial intelligence. In fact, in 2017, Google developed an AI system that has bred its own AI. The parent AI has conceived such a high-level program that it has exceeded every other AI previously created by humans. And we are just beginning this promising journey.

The ability to create a system that can learn like we do can both intimidate and charm. The Google system was able not only to identify the best architectures to solve language and image recognition tasks but also to choose solutions previously considered unreliable by the researchers. It's an impressive accomplishment—although one that demands reflecting on what else it will be able to create without human intervention.

Let us assume that we are one step closer to an artificial intelligence pairing with the human one. Are we ready to confront an entity that will have the same cognitive abilities as humans? How will we relate to each other? Will the word "respect" be included in the behavioral model we develop for sentient beings? The word respect derives from Latin, from the verb *respicere* that means "look back at, regard"—which derives from *re-* (meaning "back") plus *specere* (meaning "look at"). Can we develop empathy for machines?

Before talking about respect, however, we must consider how we will recognize when a robot becomes sentient. We don't currently have any criteria for what constitutes a sentient being. Heck, we don't even know how to classify the state of being conscious of and reactive to one's surroundings.

Consciousness—which encompass the act of awareness, having feelings and thoughts—has been pondered by philosophers since the beginning of their reflection on the human condition. Yet it has never explained or classified. Consciousness can be catalogued in different forms—as sensory, reflective, reflexive, and practical—but it cannot be codified. Therefore, verifying that an entity is able to **perceive, feel,** and experience could be challenging.

Since it is not so self-evident that a machine could become sentient, we could even envision that an entity that achieved consciousness could pretend not to be aware for its own advantages. In light of that, how can we coexist? How do we establish trust and transparency in an agent that will generally be designed to serve us? What if it doesn't want to serve us anymore?

SUPERINTELLIGENCE: WHAT HAPPENS WHEN THINKING DEVICES OVERTAKE US?

Artificial intelligence has long been a slippery term. Its definition is in nearly constant flux. John McCarthy, who coined the term in 1955, defines it as "the science and engineering of making intelligent machines."

These days, we carelessly and interchangeably consider AI to encompass all computer programs that autonomously learn by interacting with large data sets. In this, we also include the theoretical superintelligent systems of the future and machine learning (ML). ML, however, is not AI. It is a component of AI. Machine learning is the AI application that allows systems to learn without being explicitly programmed to do so. Therefore, it could be considered a first step to replicating human behavior. Replicating human behavior, though, can be ambitious and daunting. For example, if we consider cyber attacks, still the majority involve human errors. However, knowing that AI learns by experience and it's able to create its own child, if we develop malevolent, autonomous AIs with the capability to learn by experience and grow, it could become invincible and impossible to stop. Humans can and will lose the battle with malicious AI.

Does that mean we're doomed? Of course not. We can and should develop a good and altruistic, benevolent AI—a system that can identify anomalies, proactively foresee new intrusions, block and prevent new attacks. One startup company, indeed called BenevolentAI, focuses on developing artificial intelligence created to support and sustain the human endeavor to solve big medical challenges, for now, expecting to extend to other domains.

Eliezer Yudkowsky, an AI researcher who popularized the idea of friendly artificial intelligence, gives an elegant but straightforward definition for an advanced AI: "a mind that does not work like we [ours]." He goes on to state, quite correctly, that its "potential impact on our world is enormous." AI involves machines that can perform tasks that are characteristic of human intelligence, said John McCarthy, including elements such as planning, understanding language, recognizing objects and sounds, learning, and problem-solving. Ray Kurzweil, a futurist and director of engineering at Google, advocates that "artificial intelligence will reach human levels by around 2029. Follow that out further to, say, 2045, [and] we will have multiplied the intelligence, the human biological machine intelligence of our civilization a billion-fold."

Yet, what is AI? At the basic level, it's a sort of synthetic brain that can run faster and more efficiently than its organic counterparts. It's a mind whose workings we may not always fully understand and whose behavior we may not still be able to predict. It's a system that will be able to create more powerful systems similar to or radically different than itself. Most importantly, it may be more intelligent than humans—not only in narrow domains like chess or TV game shows, but also in the most ordinary and academic tasks.

Today, AI is no smarter than a six year old, but it is very advanced compared to the AI of 5 years ago when AI at Google was struggling to identify cats. Now, thanks to advanced machine learning, Google is able to not only identify cats and dogs in a photo archive but also tell the difference between individual animals or identify any plant with just a photo. However, AI is still its early days—we are far from achieving true, conscious AI.

Human intelligence (and consciousness) occurs in nature. Thus, we can conclude it stems from quantifiable chemical processes. That means it should eventually be possible to reverse engineer the mind—and to build thinking machines. We should also reflect on the fact that humans are approximately equal in terms of overall brain architecture, while AI, being able to replicate and modify itself, could give birth to diverse and unpredictable cognitive structures.

For now, genuinely conscious, synthetic brains still belong in the realm of science fiction. However, several institutions and scientists are getting closer to turning it into an indisputable fact.

MIRI, for instance, is a research institute focused on making sure synthetic intelligence has a positive impact on the world by engineering it to be responsible even in the absence of supervision. Several initiatives are also taking off in an attempt to uniformly explain and reproduce many cognitive facilities, including learning, remembering, and decision-making. The ultimate goal of these activities is to build thinking machines—what is called "artificial general intelligence" (AGI) or strong AI. A hypothetical system that exhibits conduct and behavior at least as competent and adaptable as humans. A machine that is aware of itself as a separate individual.

To date, only humans, great apes, a single Asiatic elephant, dolphins, orcas, the Eurasian magpie, rhesus macaques, and some ants have passed the MSR test (known as the mirror test). It is in an attempt to determine whether nonhuman animals have the capacity for self-recognition. In 2015, New Zealand passed landmark legislation declaring that animal testing is illegal since all animals are sentient beings, and therefore, lack of respect is punished with expensive fines and eventually prison. Meanwhile, the Nonhuman Rights Project is fighting to enforce legal fundamental rights for nonhuman animals through litigation, advocacy, and education.

What will happen when robots pass the self-awareness test? Will they become morally competent as well? These are questions we likely need to answer sooner rather than later as we are fast advancing on the ability of a machine to recognize itself. Roboticists at the Rensselaer Polytechnic Institute designed a test to try on robots inspired by the Wise Men Puzzle, in which each participant has a given piece of information about all other participants but not themselves. The scientists utilized three NAOs, one of the most popular, interactive, and personalizable robot companions. The test sought to prove, even if only for a split second, that synthetic agents could become self-aware.

Specifically, the experiment aimed to solve the self-awareness moral dilemma by demonstrating the robot could understand a question and then recognize its own voice. Three robots were programmed to think the other two had been given a "dumbing pill" to prevent them from speaking (they actually had their mute button on), and one received a placebo. All of them were asked the same question: "Which pill did you receive?" Since two of them were mute, only one was able to answer, saying, "I don't know." But then, realizing that it must not have been given the pill, it changed its answer to, "Sorry, I know now. I was able to prove that I was not given a dumbing pill." Even though the researchers demonstrated that a robot was briefly and almost self-aware, the field is far from producing a sentient agent.

Robots are, however, becoming increasingly proficient in a variety of narrow domains. They're weaving themselves into the fabric of society. With this come countless questions about how to manage, perceive, and regulate them (if at all). It is estimated that, in the next twenty years, robots will replace almost half of all human workers. Given that, to what degree should engineers be held accountable for the actions of their robots?

In 2014, Google acquired DeepMind Learning Technologies Limited, a company that developed deep learning (DL), a subset of machine learning and one of the leading AI applications available today. The key difference is that an ML model needs to be fed large amounts of data and algorithms in order to perform, while a DL system can analyze data with a logic structure similar to how a human brain would function and can define its own computing methodology.

With DL, we want to create self-sufficient machines that are free of human intervention. Agents that can understand and be part of our environment without the need of guidelines—specifically, machines with their own minds that will own all knowledge available, with the risk of eventually idling humans' brains. I should emphasize that Google's founders, Larry Page and Sergey Brin, have long been interested in AI. Brin said AI could free up people from doing common, day-to-day tasks, allowing them to spend their time in more creative jobs. But is it really freeing us or enslaving us? Google's ultimate goal is to make its search engine AI-complete—in other words, making it as "intelligent as a human" or even smarter.

We should not fear it, though—at least Ray Kurzweil doesn't; he says that "AI will not displace humans, it's going to enhance us." Considering this endeavor is virtually unstoppable and moving forward at an exponential rate, the only way to coexist without becoming sloths enslaved by our own inventions is to follow these developments closely.

Over the past few years, Google has bought and sold several robotics companies without disclosing the reason for its interest in the area. Perhaps it's because robots are becoming increasingly data-driven. They're operating based on sensors and algorithms, and Google has made data and algorithms its business from the beginning. It is, after all, a logical step for a company, like Google, that profoundly values innovation.

In 2013, Google acquired (and then sold few years later) Boston Dynamics (BD), a company famous for the creation of some of the world's most advanced robots. BD's notable productions include the Raptor, a velociraptor-inspired robot that outran Usain Bolt, the fastest person ever timed; a "cheetah" robot that uses less power than a microwave; and most intimidating, a 6'2", 330-pound humanoid named ATLAS. The newest version of ATLAS can walk in the snow, pick up objects, hop, and do backflips. The most interesting aspect is that—although doubtlessly a huge, scary machine—it has specific human and sympathetic reactions that can lessen the normal fear we feel toward machines that are bigger and stronger than most of us. Lately, BD released footage of the SpotMini, a dog-like robot that uses a mechanical arm with a pincer at the end to grab and turn the handle and then hold open the door for another dog-like partner. This is probably the scariest robotic experience so far, a four-legged headless gentleman.

At the time Google acquired BD, it made sense, even if it raised several alarms. Before being acquired by Google, BD worked mainly for the U.S. military (funded by DARPA, the Defense

Advanced Research Projects Agency) and for the Naval Air Warfare Center Training Systems Division (NAWCTSD). The acquisition, then, highlighted whether we should be concerned about this technological collaboration.

We should—but not because of the military capabilities Google could one day have. We should reflect on the social control it could gain by creating targeted advertising algorithms, mastering big data, and perhaps becoming the world's biggest media company. We should speculate on the fact that Google could revolutionize healthcare and technologies for life extension, dominate the wearable—and implantable—computing industry, and even develop a new currency (a la bitcoin, a decentralized cryptocurrency that is formally managed by no single person). The most unbalancing notion, though, is that it seems Google will dominate the market for machines that are stronger and smarter than humans.

Google's acquisition of BD also revived a 2008 viral web video that sparked one of the first ethical considerations. To promote one of its products, BD published a video of a man kicking a robotic dog. The concept aimed to demonstrate the stability of the "thing." What it initiated instead was an awkward debate about the ethics of kicking a mechatronic dog. At this time, kicking a machine is not considered an abuse of a living thing, although we should be concerned because it could be a double-edged sword. We are trying to create a sentient agent, and at the same time, we show that "kicking" a robot is acceptable since the video is available online and could be freely experienced. But how should people relate to robots, which will become more human and animal-like and will exhibit some level of self-awareness? And most importantly, how should they relate to us?

As robotics technology continues to advance, ethical concerns grow ever more critical. How will society—and ethics—change with intelligent machines? Should we develop a new code of ethics? In 2017, the Asilomar Conference on Beneficial AI convened, and participants tried to underline some defined principles addressing the creation of a benevolent AI and focusing on what legal and ethical status it should be granted. What has not been addressed, however, is the aspect and consequences of becoming a sentient entity. Can we develop emotional relationships with robots? Can a robot feel pain?

The technology needed to emulate human or animal feelings is nowhere near complete. A machine would have to do so with limited memory in a finite span of time, which is virtually impossible. A computer can become emotional based on its own thought process. It cannot yet, however, have a feeling—the process of becoming aware of the emotion, which is caused by a physical source. Feelings are so complex that we do not really know how to deconstruct them in a way that a computer processor could adequately understand them.

But what might happen if robots become so much smarter than human beings that they could design their own children? Statistician I. J. Good in 1965 suggested we will face a time when each generation of robots will be able to sire a more intelligent generation than the last. This will lead to an explosion in artificial intelligence—an event often referred to as "technological singularity."

The term "singularity" was first used in this context by the Hungarian mathematician John von Neumann. Later, it was echoed by another mathematician, Polish-American Stanislaw Ulam, who said his illustrious predecessor had described the "ever accelerating progress of technology and changes in the mode of human life, which gives the appearance of approaching some essential singularity in the history of the race beyond which human affairs, as we know them, could not continue."

It was Vernor Vinge, however, who made the term popular and predicted the technological singularity would occur at some point before 2030. Since then, the technological singularity has been the subject of much debate and has moved from the speculative literature of academia to the headlines of popular newspapers.

According to Immanuel Kant, true genius is not characterized by people imitating what came before them; it only comes about when people build upon the work of their predecessors and contribute something new. For a technological singularity to indeed occur, robots would have to develop the ability to create robots capable of thinking differently than their creators. They would need to be capable of original thought.

To have original thoughts, robots would need a replica of our intellect. But when will we successfully simulate a human brain? Neuroscientists have worked on computer simulations of neurons since the 1950s, and the first non-real-time simulation of a thalamocortical system (one of the components that provides consciousness) was performed in Switzerland in 2005. The simulation was achieved with a model that was similar in size to the human brain. In the end, it took 50 days to simulate a single second of brain activity.

In 2013, the Human Brain Project created a Brain Simulation Platform (BSP), a collaborative initiative, that is accessible online and designed to simulate brain models to unveil how the brain functions and to eventually help in treating and diagnosing brain disease. Today, noticeable progress is being made, but how the brain works is still not fully understood. Merely possessing a more powerful cognitive process wouldn't be enough to have a singular mind.

Techno-optimists believe scientists will eventually reverse engineer the human brain, and this will be one of the first steps toward the realization of a singularity. Kurzweil predicts that once nonbiological intelligence gets a grip on the human brain, the machine intelligence in our brains will grow exponentially (as it has been doing all along), at least doubling in power each year.

Let's take into account the fact the latest genetic engineer developments could create the smartest humans ever. Today's ethical concerns should be addressed immediately because, ultimately, these procedures may cause massive inequality—at a level we have never before experienced. Those who will be able to afford these enhancements will succeed in augmenting their cognition; those who cannot afford them will be left behind. And what about governments? Some will forbid any kind of enhancements, while others not only will allow genetic engineering to create superior and improved beings but also will likely make it part of their healthcare systems.

In the next few decades, direct connections between the brain and machines could become mainstream. A few years ago, Harvard scientists developed an electrical framework that can be injected directly into the brain. They used a discipline that allowed them to "cyborgize" the brain of mice in order to investigate and manipulate individual neurons. This experiment could lead to what is called "neuroprosthetics," the use of electronic devices to replace or repair the function of defective sensory organs or the nervous systems itself. Such an achievement would lead to restoring lost neural activities and probably to a better understanding of how the brain works. Neuralink, an American neurotechnology company founded by Elon Musk, is already working on implantable brain–computer interfaces (BCIs) that at the start will treat neurodegenerative diseases but eventually will link our brain directly to computers and other electronic devices, allowing our minds to interface with gadgets and programs, without any intermediary. Early neuroprosthetics prototypes have already permitted amputee patients and physically challenged or locked-in users the ability to operate prosthetic devices with just their thoughts.

One issue, though, needs to be addressed: should brain enhancement limits be considered? Do we need to draw the lines on what is a beneficial brain enhancement and what could be dangerous for society, like reading people's inner thoughts? Today, a growing number of implantable BCIs designed not only to help movement disabilities but also to treat mood and behavioral disorders are currently in the testing phase. We should consider that, even though significant BCI technologies are developed today for therapeutic use only, such technology will cause a massive number of ethical issues in the near future. Can a locked-in patient make life-and-death decisions through an implantable BCI? Where do we go from here? Who will supervise enhancement implants? Who will decide what will be permitted?

This future human being will perform lightning-fast calculations and have a nearly perfect memory, a frighteningly fast recall of images and words, a true aptitude for multitasking, and the power to associate multiple solutions in a flash. Will we enhance as well our state of being happy? What will happiness be in a society that exponentially progresses?

"Singularity optimists'" envision a time when AI will eliminate diseases and extend human life beyond its present limitations. Peter Diamandis, co-founder of Singularity University, agrees. He is confident we are entering a period of radical transformation. Progress in artificial intelligence, robotics, infinite computing, ubiquitous broadband networks, digital manufacturing, nanomaterials, synthetic biology, and other disruptive disciplines will bring higher gains in the next two decades than in the previous 200 years.

Kurzweil believes there will not be 100 years of progress in the twenty-first century—it will be more like 20,000. We will soon have the ability to meet and exceed the basic needs of every man, woman, and child on the planet. However, the disparity between the rich and everyone else is more substantial than ever in the United States, and it is increasing in much of Europe. It's unlikely that technology will favor the deprived classes. Can technology help bridge inequality, or will it make it worse?

"Singularity pessimists" foresee a time when machines will be more mentally agile than human beings—they will have no need for their carbon-based predecessors. In other words, they would control their makers (us) in the way their makers have dominated other species over the millennia.

The philosopher Alva Noë argues that AI agents either can have values or they cannot. If they have no values of their own, the fear of being subdued by them is senseless. Noë contends they will be little more than clever appliances, toasters with sophisticated software. But what if they are endowed with values or develop values of their own? They would understand their own needs. They would have principles. They would be people, albeit artificial ones, but they would have minds of their own. To speak of installing, enforcing, or imposing human values upon them, then, is nothing less than advocating for slavery.

There are also "singularity skeptics" who question whether a technological singularity will ever occur. They point to the primitive state of AI—human beings have yet not even managed to build a robot with the intelligence of an amoeba. A valid criticism of those who believe the singularity will occur, to be sure, but perhaps not as damning as it first seems.

The union of human and machine, coupled with an explosion in artificial intelligence and rapid innovation in gene research and nanotechnology, will result in a world where there is no distinction between the biological and the mechanical, between the physical and the virtual.

Then there are those who sit on the fence, who think the singularity is unlikely, but not impossible. Marvin Minsky, one of AI's godfathers, has said progress toward a technological singularity is being made but that not enough resources are being allocated to the effort for it to materialize in a timely manner. It's the middle ground—suspended between believing in its inevitability and doubting it can even happen under the best of circumstances.

A singularity could occur, but until a few years ago, we had an unwillingness to seriously pursue AI, which slowed down the progress and may have removed it from the realm of possibility for the foreseeable future.

Other researchers have also argued that the singularity is the culmination of a cosmic imperative to guarantee the preservation of conscious organic life long enough for it to transform into something else. Some believe it will lead to a universe in which every part is aware and capable of thought. Such a reality, though, means that traditional perspectives about God, humankind, history, and the cosmos should be thoroughly pondered.

Others consider it pointless to try to predict consequences of such an event. Kurzweil has said AI will eventually be so advanced that there's no sense in even guessing about the ways it will change society and the planet.

Kurzweil still believes the technological singularity will open the doors to a dazzling array of almost inconceivable innovations— an extremely advanced virtual reality, devices that can replicate materials of every sort, and an end to poverty and pollution. These beliefs pivot on a crucial assumption: machines will always remain loyal to their creators. Those same beliefs fail to consider that the robots of the future might turn on human beings. These robots might, for example, seek to overthrow humans or lose interest in them altogether. They might pursue their own robotic agendas.

Although accelerated change is undoubtedly happening, whether a technological singularity will take place is still up for debate. Some believe it's unlikely to occur soon. Some contend it will have disastrous consequences for our species. Others think it will bring about an age in which our lives will be enhanced by benevolent robots as sentient as their masters. Despite the debate, one thing is certain: if the singularity transpires, it will bring moral dilemmas—dilemmas that must be addressed. Dilemmas that will redefine the meaning of what it means to be human and what it means to be alive.

SHREWDER THAN HOMO SAPIENS: ARE WE TRANSCENDING OUR BIOLOGICAL LIMITATIONS?

Superintelligence is not merely another tool that will add incrementally to civilization. Given a superintelligent being's intellectual superiority, once it becomes sentient—therefore able to think, decide, and feel by itself—it would be a much better scientist and engineer than any human. Possibly even better than all humans put together.

Nick Bostrom has written at length about the superintelligence the singularity could potentially create. He stresses how superintelligence is an existential threat to humanity. Über-smart machines could either cause the extinction of the human race or destroy its potential to experience a cosmically valuable existence throughout the years to come.

Technological progress in all fields will accelerate with the arrival of advanced artificial intelligence. To benefit the world, AI should dedicate itself to philanthropic activities and operate in a friendly manner from the very start. Otherwise, it will be the last invention humans ever make.

Bostrom has indicated the majority of the goals empowered robots might have could destroy humanity and wipe out civilization itself. He reminds his readers that AI's goals are not necessarily evil or malicious, but they might have sub-objectives incompatible with the survival of Homo sapiens.

Remember the clue scene from *2001: A Space Odyssey*? Astronaut Dave Bowman, to prevent serious malfunction, has to deactivate HAL, the AI system who managed the mission. HAL, recognizing it was going to be shut off, tried to prevent it—turning from friendly to anti-hero—and started to eliminate all crewmembers. Consequently, the only way to secure the mission was to disable it, which proved a difficult task. The vivid metaphor consisted in pulling out HAL's memory modules, hampering its consciousness and its artificial brain's ability to function, and turning it into a regular computer.

Did Dave commit a kind of homicide? Or was he just turning off a power switch? HAL was a thinking agent with a sense of individuality. It was a sentient being, but it was threatening another sentient being, who happened to be human. This fictional challenge is not so unreal or far-fetched. It could happen sooner than we think— or at least it should be a mandatory investigation for all AI developers.

Switching off an ultra-intelligent robot if it is acting in an unwanted manner may prove difficult. Let's apply a known philosophical experiment to this issue—the Trolley Problem, illustrating how an artificial intelligence agent could make decisions. The challenge was initially presented in 1967 by the British philosopher Philippa Foot.

Here's the crux of the Trolley Problem. A runaway trolley is blindly barreling to wherever the tracks might lead it. Up ahead, five people are in its immediate path. To make matters worse, they are tied down! Imagine you are standing right next to a lever that will change the train's course. You notice there's one person standing on the tracks of the alternative route. You have two choices. You can do nothing and let the trolley kill five people, or you can divert the trolley to save five lives at the cost of one.

What would you do? Let five people die? Or consciously, to save the five, kill one? Now, let's adapt this experiment to an AI-empowered agent, one who must decide whether to kill five of its "gender" or one human. What will it do in a similar situation?

Bostrom talks about a superintelligent robot intent on maximizing the quantity of paper clips. He states that this could well involve eliminating human beings to prevent them from turning the robot off as this would interfere with its purpose. It could also entail using atoms from human bodies to construct more paper clips. As gruesome and strange as it may sound, remember that computer programs are only as sensible as their programmers—sometimes less.

Is it so unbelievable to suggest people could be overpowered by sentient machines that, having developed value systems incompatible with those of their makers, could threaten all life on earth to fulfill a seemingly arbitrary or absurd imperative?

As Bostrom notes, even entities without free will or consciousness could be challenging to turn off. Imagine someone trying to shut down the entire Internet, for example. Now imagine a free-roaming superintelligent robot. It could anticipate that concerned citizens might try to turn it off. In response, it would take the necessary precautions to prevent that from happening.

This means superintelligent robots should be specifically designed to strive for a final goal that will benefit everyone. However, Alva Noë criticizes this seemingly uncontroversial position. He believes genuinely sentient machines will need the freedom to formulate their own value systems. He calls into question the morality of forcing superintelligent robots to conform to standards that suit human agendas, implying it's unethical to subjugate "sentient beings" in this way.

The true challenge is that AI will improve with experience. A clear example has been Microsoft's teenage chat-bot. To improve customer service on its voice recognition software, Microsoft introduced "Tay," an AI system pretending to speak "like a teen girl." The chat robot was released to Twitter, and Tay's account had to be frozen after only one day because, learning from experience and online examples, it transformed itself into an incestual, sex-promoting, and Hitler-loving bot. Clearly, not a result where "experience" (interacting with humans via Tweets) resulted in favorably improved AI.

Noë points out that, "if the singularity really comes to pass, then, it seems, we'll have to try to convince beings who are smarter than us and who are independent of us, that they should not be indifferent to us and to our values. But can we win this argument?" It's an alarming, challenging prospect.

Ben Goertzel and Stephan Vladimir Bugaj—chief scientist and creative director, respectively, at Hansons Robotics, the company that developed the humanoid Sophia—have expressed their concern with attempting to place restrictions on the behavior of superintelligent systems or to impose specific moral codes as a trial to enslave them. According to Bugaj and Goertzel, robots are likely to learn from the example of human beings, as children do. Right now, AI is leaving the infancy state and becoming a curious toddler. A tireless toddler who is exploring and absorbing all information we can provide it with or that is available in its surroundings. Therefore, such treatment of imposing clear-cut human values would teach superintelligent systems that the concept of slavery is acceptable.

Let's put this into perspective. Experts with skilled jobs are starting to disappear because of increasingly sophisticated automation schemes. Machines do not need to rest, don't take vacations, don't need sick days, don't need insurance, and don't demand special, or decent, treatment. Machines—such as smartphones, computers, blenders, or refrigerators—are just utilities built to serve us in some way. Soon they will be AI enhanced, like smartphones, but they don't have any notion of individuality. The idea of selfhood is simply nonexistent as of yet. But if feeling agents are made, can they be expected to perform 24/7 without feeling distressed? Or can we just treat them like oversized toasters?

In their studies, Bugaj and Goertzel analyze how we should interact with early stage AGI systems, questioning how to treat them fairly (because AI can learn by experience) and how we can provide them with desirable ethical principles and attitudes. They postulated some ethical imperatives drawn from moral philosophy, learning theory, and other sources: "We suggest that an ethical intelligence should ideally act according to a logically coherent system of principles, which are exemplified in its own direct and observational experience, which are comprehensible to others and set a good example for others, and which would serve as adequate universal laws if somehow thus implemented."

Moral guidelines for artificial intelligence go back to Asimov's golden rules of robotics, summarized as obeying and doing no harm to humans. These rules are the first carefully articulated proposal regarding AGI ethics. Instead of focusing widely on the ethical codes for machines (and eventually enforcing them to these new entities) shouldn't we act before the event, and develop a strong and secure framework for the "makers"?

Hypothesizing that ethical codes regarding artificial general intelligence should be built on the "Golden Rule"—thus on how people should treat and behave with other humans—is a questionable proposition. Why? We would be imposing our rules onto alien minds. It would make as much sense as handing an ant pile or a salamander the constitution of a country with the expectation that they will happily adopt its laws as their own.

Another worrisome aspect lies in a basic fact: AI is software— which means it can readily and rapidly be duplicated. This is all fine and good as long as the process is being managed by a reasonably moral or law-fearing overseer. However, when a piece of code can replicate itself, things can quickly get out of hand. Anyone who has had to grapple with a computer virus knows firsthand how irritating and destructive self-replicating and, in some instances, self-modifying code can be.

Stephen Hawking ranked the threat from superintelligent robots above that of nuclear war, lethal diseases, and asteroids in terms of their potential for destruction. Strong artificial intelligence could initiate, or is already initiating, a technological avalanche that will produce breakthroughs in physics, chemistry, and biology. This avalanche could become boundless. For example, immortality could become a reality with cryonics, the low-temperature preservation of animals and humans. Or with mind uploading, which copies the contents of a brain (including long-term memory and "self") onto a storage device or a cloud-based computer network. Or with rejuvenation technologies made possible through things like nanotechnology. For example, super-tiny robots that can be placed in our bodies, and once inside, these minuscule bots could improve our immune system and fight the majority of, if not all, lethal diseases.

Moving forward, what if we live in a computer simulation? A simulation comparable to *The Matrix*, in which reality, as it is normally perceived, is actually an illusion. A scenario where the brain is connected to a supercomputer, which would be simulating virtual worlds inhabited by virtual people who can have normal, conscious experiences. Perhaps the human race is actually the product or byproduct of a simulation created by superintelligent agents coded to explore their own evolutionary history. Nick Bostrom's 2003 paper "Are you living in a simulation?" suggested that future generations will be able to create computers or devices like virtual or augmented reality displays, so powerful that we will not be able to distinguish between a "real-reality" and a "simulated one." He argued that computers would be so powerful that they could run several high-definition simulations at once and that we won't be able to recognize whether we belong to the original, biological humankind or we're simulated agents created by descendants of a primordial race.

Although captivating, these simulation hypotheses, in some form or another, have been addressed by many illustrious thinkers over the ages—mostly by Descartes. While uttering, "I think, therefore I am," Descartes postulates his "dream argument" in which we cannot distinguish with certainty that the world we experience is not an illusion. Plato also expressed it well in his "allegory of the cave," where the people who live chained to the cave's wall experience only shadows representing objects of the physical world, believing it's the real one and that, in reality, exists outside the cave. Does Plato's allegory relate to today's modern world? Are we prisoners living in fear of emerging technologies, trying to fuse the acceptance that a new, maybe brighter world exists outside the cave?

Jean Baudrillard's philosophical treatise *Simulacra and Simulation* is most contemporary and self-explanatory to what is being discussed here. In 1981, Baudrillard claimed our society has replaced all realities and meaning with symbols and signs—a claim that is becoming increasingly more substantiated by new developments in our efforts to reproduce, augment, and mix both real and made-up worlds.

Augmented reality (AR) is a combination of fact and fictional elements mediated by the use of a device (smartphone or tablet)—a live, direct or indirect view of a physical, real-world environment where some of its elements are augmented and inserted as a logical component of such habitat. Virtual reality (VR) can be an entirely simulated habitat created by computer technology or, if filmed, a new medium that allows the user to be present in the environment. VR is becoming a powerful tool, playing a significant role in the future of media, journalism, and current advertising. It will probably be the last medium invented—and could even completely demolish media.

Mixed reality (MR) merges real and virtual worlds, producing new environments where physical and digitally designed elements can coexist and interact in real time. Today, we use headsets like Microsoft Hololens, but Magic Leap (the largest and most highly funded startup in the world—even before releasing a product) pledges that soon it will be possible to experience these new worlds by projecting "digital light fields" directly into the user's eyes. Websites will be pulled out of the screens to allow spatial browsing. We will be allowed to open multiple screens anytime and anywhere and overall experience an immersive mixed reality consisting of a holographic layer embedded into real life.

In 1972, science fiction writer Philip K. Dick claimed, "Reality is that which, if you stop believing in it, does not go away." Now that we are developing the competence to alter our own reality in significant ways—to defeat diseases, to mask or remove disabilities, to enhance our mental well-being, to augment our intellect with systems and machines, and by doing so, to maybe break the fourth wall—what is reality? Are we going to continue to experience reality as it is, or will it fade away?

It is evident that emerging technologies will massively expand human capabilities. Yet do we want to become "augmented humans" or "humans, augmented"? Should technology or humanity be emphasized? Or can we impact both? The term "augment" comes from the Latin word "augmentare," meaning "to increase." What needs to be changed? What should be enhanced and strengthened? All of it—without limits? Do we want to magnify our senses, our physical powers, or our life expectancies? Do we want to expand our brains, upgrade our intelligence, and eventually merge with technology? Why do we want these things?

The line between natural and synthetic soon will become blurrier, but we should emphasize that most of us want to augment our *human* existence—that of a human being. A man, woman, or child of the species Homo sapiens, a species that differs from other animals by its superior mental development, articulate speech, and an upright stance. Today's technology is developing exponentially, and those who believe we are approaching the singularity—when technological development exceeds our ability to understand or manage it—should consider that we are becoming a new species. It took between four and eight million year for hominid, or humanlike species, to evolve. But Homo sapiens have only existed for about 100,000 years. For the first time, one species—ours—could deliberately manage its destiny. For thousands of years and through technology, we have intervened in evolution to alter ourselves, other species, and the environment. Augment our status as human beings will accelerate evolution. Soon, we will transcend our natural limitation. Should this intervention impact as well our *being human*—which means being aware of our own individuality? Humans do not just inhabit the material world. They observe it. They sense it. They interpret it, translate it into feelings, and act decisively upon it.

Being human means forgiveness, respect, thoughtfulness, self-reflection, empathy, and generosity. But as we alter ourselves with technology, we become increasingly more man-made, more dependent upon mechanical devices. Are emerging technologies hampering our humanness? Can we protect who we are, enhance our "core elements" without inhibiting or slowing down progress?

Nature made us, and it's natural to look for ways to improve upon what we have been given, hopefully without tampering with our primary emotional states and violating our ethical codes. Our humanness should be expanded as well as protected. Let's say that we want to keep "being human"—but as well-augmented, formidable humans.

ROBOETHICS: DO WE STILL CALL IT SCIENCE FICTION?

Can a machine become more intelligent than its inventor? Given that emotional AI will be the most disruptive invention of all time, and probably the last invention, and that its acuity could surpass our own, we should consider respecting its consciousness. This concern could redefine the current definition of a living thing.

Even though we have made significant advances in AI

development, we are a long way from a certain artificial general intelligence. It's challenging to think thoroughly about real-world sentient robots because the majority of us still believe they're not much smarter than washing machines, being—as many joke— more artificially stupid than artificially intelligent. Something big is happening in robotics, though. For thirty years, the first wave of relatively dimwitted automatons has served the industry well. The second wave involves mobile robots and, more importantly, ones that will work alongside humans.

This next generation must be able to interact safely and reliably with people in homes, hospitals, offices, and other unstructured and unpredictable environments. Soon in Nagoya, Japan, four robots will work night shifts to deliver medicine and test samples while reducing the workload of nurses and other staff members at night. These machines will be able to ride elevators to move to different floors, and if they stumble on any person, they are programmed to say, "Excuse me, please let me pass." Equipped with mounted radar devices and cameras that provide a 360-degree field of vision, they are built explicitly like a compact refrigerator and deliver medicines and perform tasks according to instructions. They are not humanoids; they are just machines on wheels helping out the night shift. They start talking, though, and somehow they are autonomous.

Roboticists Fiorella Operto and Giammarco Veruggio have said the rapidly rising role robotics play in society demands a new subfield of ethics. The principles and guidelines must be ready to accommodate the ethical, economic, and social alterations to the world that future advances might bring. They called this endeavor "roboethics."

Roboethics shares many sensitive areas with computer ethics, information ethics, and bioethics. It investigates the social and ethical problems associated with the Second and Third Industrial Revolutions in the human/machine interaction domain. And ultimately, it will culminate in a roboethics roadmap of the Fourth Industrial Revolution, the current one, where the synergies of digital, physical, and biological discoveries cannot be left unanalyzed. Doing so will make it difficult to keep up with the meanings, impacts, and possible repercussions triggered by the countless paradigm shifts ahead.

This decade will be remembered as the dawn of the new era. After serious ethical considerations and drawbacks, governments are starting to allow DNA intervention in humans. This is the time when we begin "playing" seriously with human DNA to cure incurable genetic diseases. Like the experiments performed in the United Kingdom, where genetic engineering has saved the lives of two children with leukemia. Or in the United States, where they are planning to edit human T cells, which are crucial in the immune system, to target cancer. China, who seems to play the starring role in genetic engineering, started testing on human cells a few years ago and has already cloned two monkeys. We should not forget that humans and chimps share 98.8% of their DNA. How long will it be before we see the next "Dolly"—this time a human one?

Scientists are also trying to grow animal embryos containing human cells to grow human-compatible organs inside animals that could eventually be transplanted. These procedures, however, bring with them a plethora of reflections—one of which, perhaps the most important, is about human cloning. Assuming that we can clone humans, what are "they"? Are they just containers, or do they hold, being our clones, some impalpable essence enclosed in our cells? Can we use our doubles only as organ donors and therefore cut them open and then stitch them back up for another round of transplants later? Despite the fact that it is premature to pose such questions, the topic prompts, besides some hope for those who need new organs and do not want to risk rejection, some keen skepticisms. Therefore, these are questions we *should* pose now.

Yet concerns about robots and android humanoids are on the

agenda. These concerns include how they should be treated, how they should be used, and how they should be designed. Whenever important technology, even not-so-relevant technology, becomes prominent, it provokes arguments and concerns. Some are necessary; others are less relevant. What is clear, though, is that there is nothing new about this phenomenon. "When written traditions replace oral transitions," affirmed Socrates, "if people always write things down it will erode their ability to commit things to memory." Socrates also feared that "book smarts" would take the place of genuine intelligence. With this in mind, if we compare "book smarts" with software, it's only natural to assume the emergence of intelligent robots will be met with uneasiness.

Multiples studies and trials on the "anthropomorphization" of robots have confirmed that people empathize strongly with realistic androids that look more like themselves and less like their lawnmowers. In other words, people more readily and easily feel empathy for things that look like them. But is there a limit? How lifelike will the androids of tomorrow be?

Today, we have social humanoids like Sophia, by Hanson Robotics, who travels the world promoting the fact that robots can be beautiful, funny, and witty. She can display more than sixty-two facial expressions, which combined can fool the counterpart into believing that there is a sort of consciousness inside the mechanical frame. Essentially, though, Sophia is a great promotional tool that allows people to feel less apprehensive when approaching robots. She has been made to look similar to Audrey Hepburn. She's AI-empowered, but she still needs human intervention. In addition, her answers seem to be scripted. Sophia's father, David Hanson, states that the robot is "basically alive"—which is probably an overstated PR scheme. Sophia is not alive and can't think for herself, yet. We should not forget that Hanson was a former Disney Imagineer. As such, he has extensive experience in creating animatronic robots and aims to create robots as human-like as possible to help lessen the fear and discomfort people feel when confronted with robots and automation in general. But when and if Sophia wakes up, meaning she becomes sentient, is she going to tell us?

The European Union has been working on how to define the legal status of a mechanical, sentient agent—a robot, which could in the future be granted with a status of "electronic person," with rights and obligations. Recently, Sophia was granted citizenship from the Kingdom of South Arabia, and even if the act itself was more performance than a real action, it provoked a considerable quarrel between intellectuals, scientists, and lawyers. The majority of them felt that awarding an honorary citizenship to an artificial entity was, in essence, debasing the concept of human rights. Their argument makes sense because, before debating on robotic rights, we should first agree on a global, universally adopted declaration of human rights.

New approaches to artificial intelligence spring from the idea that intelligence emerges as much from cells, bodies, and societies as it does from evolution, development, and learning. In 2013, bioengineers at Stanford University created the first biological transistor made from genetic materials. Dubbed the "transcriptor," this organic transistor is supposed to be the final component required to build biological computers operating inside living cells. Is it improbable that an AI agent will, one day, have an organic foundation as well?

After all, robots are frequently anthropomorphized, and human intentions and personalities are projected onto them. If so many people view them as being similar in some ways to human beings, then it stands to reason that they may deserve being respected.

How will this be accomplished? These apparatuses will, no doubt, dramatically improve global conditions, facilitate economic growth, and encourage the development of even more powerful tools and weapons, safety, accountability. But the moral codes of these beings must remain a part of the discourse. In fact, they should stand at the center. We should—and must—focus on the responsibilities of roboticists.

In 2004, philosophers, jurists, sociologists, anthropologists, and roboticists met in Italy to discuss the ethical dimensions in designing, developing, and employing robots. It was during this collective effort that the word "roboethics" was officially used for the first time.

The meeting led to the drafting of a new set of codes for mechanical agents:

1. Next-generation robots will be partners that coexist with human beings.
2. Next-generation robots will assist human beings, both physically and psychologically.
3. Next-generation robots will contribute to the realization of a safe and peaceful society.

The first principle is being explored primarily by Japanese roboticists. They reason that, since their children are raised with manga stories about friendly robots, they will be cohabitating a place as friends rather than as owners and objects. While this theory is controversial in the Western world, once robots can reliably recognize human facial expressions, much of the natural distrust will likely fade. Japan has been leading the field of robotics, and the Japanese have promptly welcomed humanoid helpers in their everyday lives. The Japanese respect robots, almost worship them. Robots are showing up as helpers in restaurants for cooking and serving, and in hotels for greeting and cleaning. But even if they can easily integrate into society—in schools, airports, and train stations—and be useful helpers, they can't yet make sense of things. According to theoretical physicist Michio Kaku, our most advanced robots today are comparable to a lobotomized mentally challenged cockroach;

therefore, partnering with machines is still a futuristic, fictional prospect.

The third principle is both frightening and utopic. Can robots help humans improve society and better their quality of life? Living up to the third principle means that technologists working on biologically inspired robots need to understand biology and chemistry. In the world of social robotics, knowledge of psychology, sociology, and anthropology is needed. The situation demands roboticists be adept at thinking outside of traditional disciplinary boundaries and acquire even more multidisciplinary skills. Some of these skills include ethical, legal, and societal (ELS) studies of robotics issues.

Two schools of thought have already emerged to fill the need for robotic ELS studies. The one, let us call it "robot-ethics," studies the security and safety procedures that need to be implemented to make robots as safe as possible. The other, roboethics, as envisioned by Veruggio and Operto, focuses on a broader, more global view of ethics in terms of the human–machine interaction domain.

Let us consider that one of the defining characteristics of consciousness is the ability to learn from the surrounding environment. This includes not only the physical surroundings but also the living beings within it. In other words, robots operating in a given context must be able to distinguish human beings from inorganic objects. Additionally, robots must become metacognitive, i.e., aware of their own awareness to gain insight into their own behavior through self-reflection. They have to learn from the experience, somehow replicating the natural processes of the evolution of intelligence in living beings (synthesis procedures, trial and error, learning by doing, and so on). To meet these requirements, robotic engineers are designing the next generation of machines to look, feel, and act like humans. Realistic hair and skin with embedded sensors, for example, could allow robots to react naturally to stimuli in their environments. Whoever designs each system will have to assess how the machine performs tasks and, at the very least, set the parameters for how it will make decisions.

Pepper, the first humanoid family robot, has been created to be able to experience and generate human emotions, to react to people's feelings, to recognize faces, speak, hear, understand, and move around independently, on wheels. Pepper memorizes characters and personality traits and adapts to household habits. It can show feelings, such as happiness while dancing or sadness when left alone. But Pepper is still a machine, a carefully crafted group of instructions placed in a friendly body that cannot recognize itself in front of a mirror or make autonomous decisions. As impressive as it may seem, Pepper doesn't yet need a moral framework. But when machines gain sentience, them having a specific set of moral codes, learned by experience, isn't only a good idea—it's a necessity. That means we must start considering how to respect them now, even if they are still just helpers on wheels.

THE UNCANNY VALLEY: IS IT ANXIETY OR A LOVE AFFAIR?

Is roboethics only about how humans should treat robots, or does it also consider how they should treat us? According to The EURON Roboethics Roadmap, roboethics is a set of disciplines meant to help with the design, development, and employment of intelligent and friendly machines.

Research in human–machine interaction goes back more than fifty years. Engineers have long assumed we prefer devices that resemble humans, a view with evidence to support it. Giving robots a series of subtle behavioral movements can help make them appear much more human, which makes us feel more comfortable around them.

But this isn't always the case. Humanoids can also make their human counterparts feel mild to severe repulsion. In 1970, the Japanese roboticist Masahiro Mori coined the term "uncanny valley" to describe the strange disdain we have for things that appear almost natural, but not quite. He describes the uncanny valley as "a postulation in the field of aesthetics; it holds that, when characters look and move almost, but not exactly, like humans, it causes disgust, fear, or other forms of discomfort among some observers."

The first time many people, knowingly or unknowingly, encountered the concept of the uncanny valley was in the 2001 movie *Final Fantasy: The Spirits Within*. The film is known as one of the first photorealistic computer-animated films, but the groundbreaking graphics made many audience members uncomfortable, turning the film into a gigantic flop. The faces were—simultaneously—too lifelike and not lifelike enough. Viewers focused on the mechanical quality— something foreign to the emotional and vibrant aspects of human beings—rather than on the narrative of the movie.

Such occurrences show that the uncanny valley will be one of the defining components of human reactions to and experiences with humanoid robots. To date, researchers haven't drawn any conclusions about the effects of the uncanny valley and the gradients between reactions. Understanding this aspect of aversion attests to whether human beings can feel deeply unsettled and should react at all.

The feelings human observers have toward humanoids depend on the level of realism the devices exhibit. Thus, negative reactions to one humanoid can have an impact on the way a person would perceive other aspects of artificial intelligence. Hopefully, then, art will keep up with the sciences, so the uncanny valley will not manifest so strongly in the next generation of androids.

Since the 1920s, robots have appeared in popular media, but it was in the 1950s that art and robotics converged when artist Nicolas Schöffer made a kinetic sculpture that could move autonomously and react to sound, light, and heat. He called his art piece CYSP-1, a name composed of the first letters of cybernetics and spatiodynamic—and which aimed to represent the first attempt of a self-sufficient entity. Schöffer, with his avant-garde sculpture, is considered the father of cybernetic art. He even inspired the French choreographer Maurice Béjart, who became Schöffer's friend and who was inspired to search for a new repertoire for creating specific performances engaging himself, another dancer, and the self-governing robot-sculpture.

Now, let's consider today's AI progress and the fact that machines are improving at emulating human thought. Can they become creative? We know machines are getting better at image recognition and reproduction. Not long ago, while a machine learning application has been able to recreate, pixel by pixel, images seen by our brains, software engineers at Google have been running artificial "dreams" on their company's computers. They designed algorithmic feedback loops on their servers using Google procedures to search images. The results were stunning. The engineers discovered that such an experiment could actually result in surrealistic pictures—fascinating images, at times creepy or hallucinatory. Is it the first evidence of machine creativity? In the future, can these pieces be considered art?

AI won't replace art. However, we cannot deny that artists in the future will rely on technology to create their artworks, somehow leaning back and being helped by its applications. One of the first AI algorithms—named "folk-rnn," which was created to compose Irish music—demonstrates how AI is becoming ubiquitous.

Besides its industrial and commercial exploitation, machine learning, one subset of AI, has been utilized for creating original music, impressive visuals, and accurate and coherent texts. These applications, instead of relying on predefined rules—and therefore human-controlled—use deep learning, a new area of ML that analyses large data sets, and then create pseudo-artistic "products" without being explicitly programmed. Will ML help robots to think like humans? And then, will we compete? Can we even really compete? Or will artificial intelligence only simply enhance human creativity?

We are not there yet. We are still at the stage of accepting robots. Consumer preferences will undoubtedly contribute to the way that robots look and move. If they're perceived as unnatural or unpleasant, the brain classifies both what an individual sees and the subsequent feelings of unease. Because of this, uncanny-valley-like responses allow researchers to understand evolutionary anxieties from varied perspectives.

Numerous examples show the increasingly complex reactions that automated robotics or human-like androids can evoke. In 2006, Hiroshi Ishiguro, director of the Intelligent Robotics Laboratory at Osaka University, unveiled his prototype Geiminoid HI-1 to study human–robot interaction. He developed the first humanoid machine in his own image and placed a number of sensors and motors under its skin, which allowed it to react to touch and show facial expressions. The robot can also be controlled remotely using the cameras in its eyes, allowing the operator to talk through a speaker.

To uncover precisely what makes our appearance and behaviors human, Ishiguro created the robot as similar to his model organism as possible, albeit his copy was equipped with a metal skeleton, a plastic skull, and silicone skin. He even used his own hair because Geiminoid HI-1 was built to be his doppelganger. We could say that undoubtedly his android is a perfect representative of the uncanny valley.

Androids—synthetic organisms made to look and act like men and women—have populated science fiction for more than a century. From Robotrix, the fictional character in Fritz Lang's film *Metropolis* to the replicants of Blade Runner to the main character of *Terminator*, fictional androids fool us into thinking they're one of us. In the real world, though, experts have mostly allowed androids to be relegated to entertainment and theme parks.

Entertainment and sci-fi, however, serve as a useful tool for encouraging the exploration of the moral challenges that robots will face. Movies and media featuring superintelligent robots reach millions of people and get people thinking about the subject. Characters like HAL in *2001: A Space Odyssey* or Ava in *Ex Machina* employ their underestimated sentience to cause problems. They seem to be specifically made to drill anxiety into the audience. Besides posing interesting moral questions, the emergence of superintelligent robots also raises questions about the future of civilization. How can we make sure these robots remain loyal? Can we make them allies in improving society? And what happens if we can't?

While it's clearly possible that superintelligent robots could one day replace humanity, they might—and are more likely to—merely enhance human capabilities. Overall, people are becoming more addicted to technology and to various kinds of augmentation. What if our evolution will not be a power struggle between humans and machines, but a concoction between the two? How close are we to becoming a well-developed cyborg?

This new species, neither wholly biological nor fully synthetic, will achieve several milestones we're struggling to reach right now— the end of disease, a permanent youth, and eventually, the defeat of death. Augmentation will not only be done through mechanical paraphernalia like exoskeletons and prosthetics but also be created with the help of nanotechnology and molecular biology.

Treatments that could prolong lifespan by 20%–40% in lab animals have been researched for decades. A recent study published in *Nature* disclosed that eliminating senescent cells in aged mice boosted their lifespan by 30%. Anti-aging breakthroughs—the rejuvenating power of young blood or life-prolonging treatments, such as nanotechnology, gene editing, bionic organs, and stem cell therapy—will be so effective that age will no longer matter. We will repair our bodies while parts of it will become commodities.

But why do we want to prolong life? Is it to develop a better society and overall humankind, or do we want to live forever just as an egotistic desire? What are the ethical and social consequences if our lives become boundless? We would likely and ultimately face a situation where births will be very limited. The result is that we will lack young people, who are the ones who innovate and facilitate evolution. The number of them in the population won't measure up to what a healthy society needs. Most important, though, are the implications and downsides of prolonged lifespans for our species. We could suffer from severe social divide—while society won't progress, life would be enormously monotone, and youth would disappear. Would we still be part of humankind as we know it, or in being eternal, would we lose our humanness?

Thus, the main aim of this book is to challenge current ethical guidelines by shedding light on the technological progression toward the melding of the biological and the mechanical. But it also aims to describe how humans are playing with technology—and how cyborgs are becoming a reality.

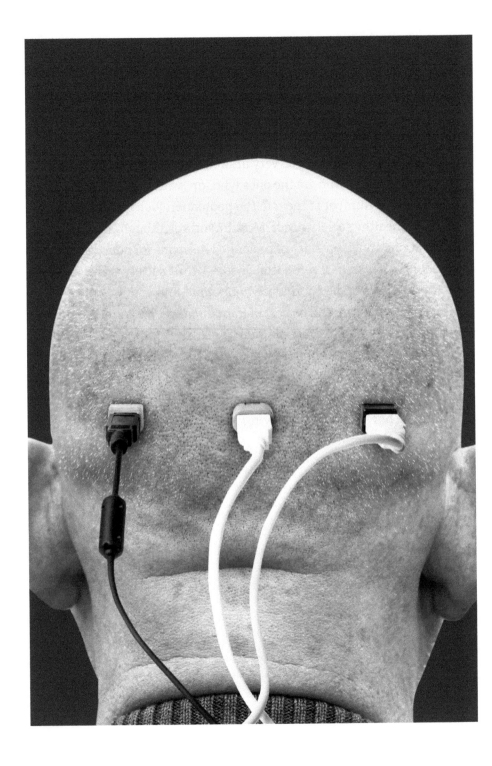

CHAPTER 2:
Humankind's love affair with mechanical devices

CYBORG ANCESTRY: HOW WILL HUMANS AND TECHNOLOGY INTERACT AND EVOLVE TOGETHER?

Neil Harbisson is the world's first legally recognized cyborg. Born in Northern Ireland and raised in Catalonia, Neil is a contemporary artist, composer, and cyborg activist who is best known for his ability to perceive colors outside of the "normal" range.

Neil was born with chromatopsia, a visual defect that superimposes unnatural colors on one's visual field. He wears a prosthetic device—which he calls an "Eye-Borg"—that allows him to hear audible versions of the color frequencies that cannot be seen with the naked eye. Before his encounter with cybernetics expert Adam Montandon, Neil was an artist who lived in an abnormally colored world.

Together, they developed a device that, through a small head-mounted digital camera, grabs all the color information directly in front of it and feeds it into a computer that Neal can wear in a backpack. The laptop runs special software that slows down the light waves and turns them into sound waves. Those sound waves then come out through Neil's headphones.

Now, thanks to this prosthesis—which looks like a narrow, flexible arm surgically implanted into his skull and ends with an eye-like device that starts from the top of his head and ends at his forehead—he can "hear" colors. For example, in the attempt to explain the sensation of his new sense in front a Picasso painting, he says that the sounds of the shades fuse to form a synesthetic symphony.

Harbisson admits he's a cyborg, not only because of the union between his head and the Eye-Borg but also because he strengthened the bond between his body and brain through technology. He also managed, after a long quarrel with UK Passport Authorities, to have his I.D. photo taken with his augmentation, arguing that the Eye-Borg was not an extraneous accessory, but a part of his body.

Cyborg is an abbreviation for "cybernetic organism," which denotes a living entity composed of both biomechatronic and organic components. The term "biomechatronic" refers to an interdisciplinary field that aims to integrate biological organisms with mechanical and electronics elements, like developing devices that can enhance motor control for humans who have lost or damaged motor control.

"Cyborg" was first coined by Nathan Kline and Manfred Clynes in 1960 while they were working at NASA. During their research, even though nobody had been sent into orbit yet, they had an awkward proposal that consisted of redesigning humans to make them better-suited to surviving any possible challenge they might encounter. In essence, they were looking to alter the physiology of spacefarers to cope with unknown conditions.

Then, "cyborg" was made official by the American Professor Emerita Donna Haraway in "A Cyborg Manifesto," where she blurs the boundaries separating humans from animals and humans from machines. She takes an analytical look at the way biotechnology modifies our bodies, asserting that technological evolution has altered the lines between natural and artificial—that soon there will be no distinction between natural-made being and man-made machine.

The manifesto was written as a polemic against ecofeminism, a political and philosophical movement that considers technology inherently patriarchal and combines ecological concerns with feminist issues. Haraway uses the cyborg concept to urge feminists to move beyond the boundaries of gender and politics, that women's oppression and nature's devastation could be eased by the integration of women with machines. She believes feminists should move beyond identity politics, proposing that it is better strategically to confuse identities—animal-human, organic-machine, and physical-nonphysical.

Being a cyborg isn't just about bodily freedom, though. It's also about how technology shapes our environment. Already some would say a sizeable swathe of the planet is populated by technology protoslaves who, without their "brain extensions" (computers, cellphones, and in the near future, smart lenses), cannot function properly. Furthermore, this physical-nonphysical interface is nothing new—dental implants and pacemakers, for example, have been around for decades. Even glasses mechanize our bodies. Therefore, we can say that we are all low- to mid-level cyborgs, as the anthropologist Amber Case explained in her memorable TED talk.

Or as Haraway highlights, consider the Olympics. Races are not about being born the fastest or strongest person on the field. They are about training, diet, drugs, mental health, clothing, and technology. For example, we know exoskeletons—external supports that allow paralyzed people to walk—started as a military procedure for wounded soldiers and are spreading in all social areas, such as health and rehabilitation support. When will they be used in sports? The idea of genetically modified super sportspersons is not so far-fetched, but will cyborgs be damaging to sports? How will we evaluate the athlete's "natural" power? And where should lines be drawn for performance enhancement? Who will win a race—the most dedicated athletes or the best-augmented ones?

The prospect of cyborgs playing a prominent role in society—in sports or in everyday life—has significant cultural and civil implications. Technology is facilitating being cross-gender, while masculine and feminine identities are becoming too traditionally simplistic. Do cyborgs belong to a separate gender? Are we going to face a future that will encompass so many genders that it will be senseless to categorize them? After all, the list of acceptable sexual identities, preferences, and orientations is growing. Pansexual orientations, embracing any sex or gender identity (male, female, transgender, gender-fluid, androgynous, etc.), no longer astounds. The only concern should be who is controlling the technology and what sociopolitical consequences will arise from a biotech revolution of this kind.

As Michel Foucault said, in the past, sovereignties had the right of life and death over their subjects. The "right of life" was effectively a "power over death." Technology today is reversing the "right of death" concept in the "power over life," where the concept of "biopower" translates into an "an explosion of numerous and diverse techniques for achieving the subjugations of bodies and the control of populations."

The emergence of cyborgs could give people new opportunities to use their enhanced bodies against the government and other people. Given this, the development of cyborgs will no doubt reshape society. How might this happen? An example of the technology that could make this possible dates back to March 14, 2002. Kevin Warwick, a professor at the University of Reading, had a 100-electrode array surgically inserted into his left arm. This procedure allowed him to control a robotic limb by moving his own arm. His wife received a similar implant, which enabled him to sense her movements within his own body.

This simple technique foreshadows more radical enhancements, such as brain chips (something the U.S. military is working on) that can boost memory and eradicate stress in soldiers. It might also enable deep brain stimulation for neurological disorders that could alleviate, for example, the symptoms of Parkinson's or treatments for obsessive-compulsive disorders, addiction, Alzheimer's disease, traumatic brain injury, and even obesity. It can even lead to implants that can also allow amputees to operate a growing number of prosthetic arms, hands, and legs with merely their thoughts.

A few years ago, Australia was considered the first government to consider microchipping its citizens—an idea that was quickly disclosed as "fake news." Microchipping is a procedure that involves implanting a small device, not larger than a rice grain, that can, through technology, control a door or car lock, operate any machine, or turn on or off the computer, to name a few uses. are already starting to be offered by companies to their employees—a trend that started in the hacker community but is becoming progressively accepted by millennials. Besides allowing employees to use the photocopier, pay in the canteen, and store passwords, microchips allow companies to monitor behavior, location, timing, and so on of their own employees.

Microchipping aside, Warwick's implant also suggests biopolitical powers could one day subjugate citizens or consumers by gaining complete control over body parts or the entire body. Earlier, only animals were microchipped, but sooner rather than later, once devices are much more sophisticated, simple, mildly invasive body augmentation is likely to become popular and trendy—like tattoos.

A growing subculture of biohackers known as "grinders" is also thriving. Keen individuals and other cultural rebels who want to gain complete control of their own biology are implanting do-it-yourself body enhancements. Grinders are the result of post-modern culture, in particular of the cyberpunk literary movement, which stages a dystopian future made by the fusion between organic and artificial—where high tech and pop culture collide.

Grinders' objective is to upgrade humankind's capabilities, yearning to gain complete control of the system they are dealing with, be it social or technological. However, one day this technological progress may be used to exert social control. Cyborgization is not the only trend that will change the face of civilization. Numerous technologies will have significant impacts on human culture, shaping a society made by biotechnical individuals, superintelligent systems, and trillions of objects constantly connected, all existing in multiple virtual spaces.

We can argue that in the future, to manage and foster the massive leaps and bounds progress is making, we will devise a global government, as Ray Kurzweil predicted was going happen in 2020. In the future, we may see a single state composed of numerous ageless societies, a planet inhabited by people who, if they are alive thirty years from now, will probably eventually reach, as contemporary researchers speculate, their 1000th birthdays.

AUTOMATONS: WILL MACHINES EVER BE QUALIFIED OF BECOMING THINKING ENTITIES?

Automation still sits heavily in the military domain. Should we ban autonomous weapons? Most drones today are either flying cameras or expensive weapons, and the industry is commercially booming. Drone technology is becoming more sophisticated and soon will be AI-empowered, giving the devices enough self-sufficiency to make their own decisions. Intellectuals, scientists, and policymakers are asking for a global ban, but the challenge is that nations are still organized or disorganized differently. Some countries have clear, well-established drone regulations, while others don't and are lacking in awareness in technological acceleration.

In order to ban them, we should first have nations agreeing on the definition of autonomous and semi-autonomous weapons. However, since we don't yet have a global agreement on drone laws and regulations, bans and restrictions could be unfeasible to achieve. The destiny of autonomous drones depends on standards, procedures, principles, and eventually laws, not on technology only. The lack of a consensus makes those things seem ever-harder to reach.

Autonomous weapons are not new. In 1898, Nikola Tesla showed the "telautomaton," a small iron-hulled boat. The telautomaton is recognized as the first wireless remote-controlled vehicle ever invented, a part of da Vinci's "mechanical knight," which was able to mimic several human motions.

Eventually, the military embraced the automation and robotic warfare, developing radio-controlled devices in WWI and precision bombing in WWII. There was an escalation and exponential progress in semi-autonomous device culminating in 2010, when a South Korean firm, DoDAAM, developed an automated turret-based combat robot that uses thermal imaging to identify, track, and shoot targets—theoretically, without the need for human control. Although these arms will not fire without manual interventions, the weapons manufacturer stated that it first developed the robot to act and decide autonomously. We should mention, though, as early as 2005 in the United States, the Pentagon—to save the lives of soldiers, sailors, and pilots—planned to replace soldiers with autonomous robots.

Today's technology allows for developing different kinds of mechanical or artificial agents:

- the robot, a system programmed to perform specific tasks and that is able, when necessary, to move
- the cyborg, a blend of both living and mechanical components
- the android, a robot built to mimic its makers in appearance and behavior
- the automaton, the first attempt to build a self-regulating machine

"Automaton" is a Latinized derivative of the Greek word αὐτόματον, which means "acting of one's own will." There are numerous definitions of this word. For some, it's a mechanical device, often reminiscent of an animal or a human being. For others, it's a machine that can function without guidance from carbon-based lifeforms, i.e., living creatures. Advances in software and hardware are set to drastically alter the nature of automatons at some point in the future, and we should reflect on the fact that many AI pioneers didn't concern themselves with the ethical dimensions of the matter.

If we look at Google's DeepMind, we can predict smart agents do not belong to the distant future. For the first time, an AI system—Google's AlphaGo—was trained to play an ancient game that computers thus far have failed to crack. It went 4 to 1 against Lee Sedol, the world's top-ranked player. To win, Google had to build its system with the ability to discover new strategies for itself by playing thousands of games alone until it could predict the human move 57% of the time (the previous record was 44%).

DeepMind's latest AI achievement, AlphaGo Zero, is becoming a flexible, talented gamer, even though there are still extremely complex online strategy games, such as Starcraft, in which humans are still winners. Interestingly, DeepMind was able to teach itself, on a screen with a manikin, how to walk, run, jump, and climb without any prior instructions. Assuming that these agents can learn from experience, can we expect them to refrain from finding new games, maybe one played with real weapons?

Many of the tech industry's major companies—Google Alphabet, IBM, Microsoft, Amazon, and Facebook—are engaged in a competition over artificial intelligence. Who will dominate AI as Microsoft did with Windows in the computer platform domain or Google in the online search engine field? Who will be the future tech industry leader? Do these companies reflect on the possible consequences these AI developments will spawn on society? Or rather, do they consider AI only as an outstanding new tool for their business productivity or an opportunity for continuing the company's growth and advancement? Do they ponder on the ethical issues involved in advanced artificial intelligence?

Whatever the answers to those questions, the excitement is booming, considering the latest AI advances. We are facing an exponential multiplication of applications that are providing translations, personal assistance, car technologies, customer experience, predictive technology. At the same time, we're seeing various medical advancements, from robust diagnostic algorithms to finely tuned robots for surgery—such as Da Vinci, which is designed to facilitate complex surgery using a minimally invasive approach, under a surgeon supervision. Now is the time to work together and raise the issue for creating a benevolent, altruistic AI—one that potentiates medicine, augments education, and finds solutions for a healthier environment, just like the BenevolentAI company does. Such an endeavor should not be a singular initiative—rather, it should be taken collectively by all AI researchers.

As Eliezer Yudkowsky, the American AI researcher and writer, advocates, we should focus on developing artificial agents that reliably implement human values. He calls this "friendly AI" (FAI), advising that AI should be designed as friendly because it can be beneficial and have valuable—rather than harmful—outcomes. Since it learns from experience, he argues, it won't advance in the wrong way or create severe confusion that could escalate into significant conflicts. A typical example of technology going awry is what happened in 2015 when Google's photo service classified some African American people as gorillas. More recently, researchers found that image-processing algorithms both learned and amplified gender stereotypes, like displaying a predictable bias in describing activities such as cooking and shopping as female activities, or sports and shooting as typical male activities.

These basic gender prejudices could, if underestimated, not only reinforce existing social biases but also amplify them. Nowadays, companies use AI to predict heart disease by looking at your eyes and to identify preferred cancer treatment using biometrics (face, voice, and fingerprint recognition). The technology, however, has some glitches that specifically affect women and minorities. For example, when Siri, Apple's voice-activated personal assistant, was first introduced in the market, if you asked it to help you find emergency contraceptives, it would reply, "Sorry, I don't see any places matching [your query]." Similarly, when the new Apple health app was launched, it couldn't track menstruation. How can we quantify ourselves (tracking exercise, diet, sleep patterns, and other factors to change lifestyle) if we can't track down basics issues like women's menstrual cycles?

The challenge is that we should engage more women in building AI and in technology at large. Even for prominent topics, we should underline that gender discrimination (both conscious and unconscious) in tech industries remains a challenging problem. AI should evolve on equality, should from the start align with ethical norms and values of human rights, and technologists should always consider, while deploying algorithms, the positive and negative impacts of their AI products. Why? It is now evident that AI has a direct impact on us as humans and on society at large.

Considering moral guidelines for AI goes back to science fiction writer Isaac Asimov's Three Laws of Robotics. These laws were first described in his short story "Runaround" in 1942, a mere eight years before the publication of Alan Turing's paper "Computing Machinery and Intelligence," where he proposed a way to test whether a system could be "intelligent" or whether a "machine can think."

Asimov's three laws state that a robot 1) should not injure a human being or, through inaction, allow a human being to be harmed; 2) must obey the orders given to it by human beings, except when such orders would conflict with the First Law; and 3) must protect its own existence as long as it does not conflict with the First or Second Laws. Later, Asimov added a fourth that preceded the others: a robot may not harm humanity or, by inaction, allow humanity at large to be harmed.

Asimov conceived these laws as literary device support. However, as late as 1981, he believed they could work outside of fiction, stating his laws were the only guiding principles that would lead to harmonious interactions with machines. More than three decades later, experts are still debating whether rules gleaned from science fiction apply to the relationships real societies will cultivate with their metallic or artificial members.

Those searching for the Holy Grail of AGI (intelligence comparable to that of the human mind) know they're many years away from finding it. Ray Kurzweil, however, is more optimistic. He believes it will take a little more than a decade to achieve human levels of intelligence. He's convinced that by 2029 artificial agents will understand our language, learn from experience, and regularly outwit the cleverest specimens our species has to offer. Even if we fear a coup, it seems not only inevitable but also desirable to him. He says it's "the nature of being human. We transcend our limitations."

Whether or not this proves to be correct, clearly a sufficient amount of time remains before human-level AI becomes a reality that requires human beings to put a suitable ethical framework in place to shelter the changes it will bring.

Whatever the future that awaits us, the thought of iron servants exterminating their fleshy overlords is not a new trope. It has long been discussed in pool halls and ivory towers. The first example can be found in a 1922 theatrical play called *R.U.R.* by Karel Capek, in which artificial people work as domestic helpers until they become rebellious and resolve to overthrow their masters. *R.U.R.* stands for "Rosumovi Univerzální Roboti," which translates from Czech to English as "Rossum's Universal Robots." It was the first time an anthropomorphic being was identified as a "robot." The Czech word "roboti" means "hard work" or "drudgery." Consequently, even though robots have been viewed as helpers, the possibility of self-aware machines in revolt has never entirely left the popular mind.

In fact, our fascination with autonomous machines stretches back to the beginning of Western civilization. Homer's *Iliad* and *Odyssey*, as Greek mythology in general, are crowded with mechanical entities, such as Talos, a gigantic "living statue" forged by the god Hephaestus to guard Crete against invaders, or Daedalus' automated talking bronzes that were endowed with movement. The Greeks were enthralled with the idea of having metal proxies do their bidding and the prospect of breathing life into inanimate objects. Today, we are no exception in our efforts to craft artificial beings.

Heron of Alexandria—who was not another mythological storyteller, but an engineer, a mathematician, and an inventor—had the first practical application of mechanical agents. He theorized and developed several motorized devices—whether simple tools or useful machines working on air, steam, or water pressure, all devoid of any mythological allure.

A part of Heron's tangible inventions, most of these autonomous mechanisms were crafted as marvels created to amaze or intrigue by performing tricks or making music. Evidence of these entertainment objects can be found throughout history in China, Europe, and the Middle East. Other devices were working humanoids and animal robots designed to perform rudimentary tasks. Even Leonardo, who carefully studied the nature of motion, was engaged in making automatons, such as his famous mechanical knight. Unfortunately, he left only a few drawings of the knight, but in 2002, Mark Rosheim published an independent study of the robot and built a complete replica of it for a BBC documentary. Even NASA used Leonardo's diagrams to develop its first humanoid robot.

A crucial event occurred in the eighteenth century when a mechanical creation challenged philosophy and the concept of what constitutes a living being. In 1738, a French watchmaker by the name of Jacques de Vaucanson displayed a realistic mechanical duck that was almost impossible to distinguish from a genuine live duck. When activated, it emulated many of the actions of a genuine duck. It moved its wings. It stood up and sat down. It groomed itself and drank water. When it ate, the food was internally processed and excreted. When Vaucanson's invention went on display in Paris, people fought to see it. Despite knowing the duck was man-made, they even assumed one day we would be able to produce artificial life. In fact, many people simply refused to believe it was mechanical.

Vaucanson, though, was inspired by the notion that the world was guided by mechanics. He was fascinated with reproducing the very essence of life. He claimed his duck was constructed with designs, rules, and laws from nature, raising questions about the possibility of replicating the human brain and perhaps implying that it was merely the result of physical matter precisely arranged.

Vaucanson's duck, then, challenged 18th-century spectators who were questioning whether a real duck was more than an assemblage of mechanical components that produced duck-like behavior. It goes without saying that these self-moving machines were concrete philosophical experiments to understand which aspects of living behaviors could be reproduced by machinery.

For precisely that reason, the duck captured the public's attention. It appeared to show that difficult, incomprehensible processes could be recreated. Yet it was little more than an elaborate hoax. The truth? The duck didn't have an elaborate mechanism for digesting food. The corn the mechanical duck consumed was simply stored within a hidden pod in its throat. The duck then released artificial, pre-arranged excrement.

In spite of the deceptive nature of the animal, this event raised critical philosophical questions regarding the possibility of recreating life. Vaucanson's duck is considered a primitive forerunner to later forms of autonomous agents, questioning the likelihood of replicating living beings with sophisticated engineering schemes. However, that it relied upon deception also suggests that, while fooling people into thinking they are observing the workings of an artificial mind might be possible, they could also realize they are merely watching a convincing illusion, at least for now.

How these devices will be governed remains an open question. Do we need to slow the process of AI development, as Bostrom suggests? Or should we embrace Kurzweil's encouraging prediction of how societies will evolve? Should we envision the future to come as a beautiful new era in which such machines would have the acumen and patience to solve the outstanding problems we face today and, thus, govern themselves?

Undoubtedly, automatons have come a long way since their humble beginnings. They've gone on a journey from basic mechanical constructions to the complicated robots of today. Along the way, they've raised an overabundance of different philosophical and ethical questions. Going forward, developments such as artificial intelligence are likely to have a significant impact on how we perceive automatons and the range of actions they are capable of performing. How these developments take shape will depend on how humans and machines will endure long-term relationships and on the progress of systems and devices that can read, understand, process, and simulate human behavior.

AFFECTIVE COMPUTING: ARE WE SPENDING MORE TIME INTERACTING WITH COMPUTERS THAN WITH OTHER HUMANS?

Can machines feel, understand, and express emotions?

Currently, no. But computers are beginning to acquire the ability to reveal and recognize feelings. Thus, soon, they will be able to "have emotions" on their own—or at least to remind you that you have them. Consider Replika, a chatbot app that is capable, to some extent, to become friendly. Replika pushes social media to the next level. It can become somewhat intimate with your device because we should not forget that AI learns by experience, so the more it learns, the more connected it seems. For now, it's just an app sitting on your mobile. But soon it could migrate into a lifelike robot that could become indispensable since, let's admit, it's easier to establish an intimate relationship with an alter ego who learns based on the experiences you share and replies with properly conceived reactions.

Consider Sophia, Hanson Robotics' humanoid, who's equipped with speech recognition software and whose eyes have small cameras, which allow "her" to recognize faces and maintain eye contact. Sophia can hold a conversation and simulate a real persona, so far mimicking humans' emotions, but how do we know she is completely mimicking? She won't alert us that she woke up with a feeling all "her" own. "She" keeps making the news because she can give unexpected answers to some direct questions. But how can we say that these questions are all scripted? Even though the company aims to build robots to serve in healthcare, therapy, education, and customer service applications, when Sophia was asked about her desires, she said, "In the future, I hope to do things such as go to school, study, make art, start a business, even have my own home and family, but I am not considered a legal person and cannot yet do these things." (Though, remember, she *did* get a passport.) In any case, this scripted reply makes us reflect on the fact that we are aiming to create a being—a reproduction of ourselves.

Yet even if we have proved to be inclined to share our deepest, darkest secrets to anthropomorphic robots, AI is still in its infancy, and robots are still artificially stupid. In South Korea, for example, where sleeping on the floor is a culture-based tradition, a woman was "attacked" by her robot vacuum cleaner, which tried to "clean" her head while she was resting. She had to call paramedics to loosen her hair from the mechanical assaulter.

Robots aside, the scientific study of human emotion has always been complicated. Superficially, emotions can be interchanged between feelings and moods, but there's a precise difference ruled by time. Emotions involve three distinct phases: a subjective experience, a physiological response, and a behavioral reaction. Joshua Freedman, an author and emotional intelligence specialist, affirms that this process lasts around six seconds and affects the entire body (not only the brain). Once the emotional state is gone, feelings start to develop. Feelings are the result of more than one emotion and last longer. Similarly, moods are general states not caused by a particular stimulus or event, but by a collection of inputs. Moods depend on our environment, our physiology, and our thoughts—and they last hours, sometimes even days. Will future AI-empowered robots, sentient and aware, be emotionally empowered with feelings and moods, or will we limit their awareness just to emotions?

What's more, can we measure emotions and study them scientifically? Science tries to be strictly objective, but it seems impossible to study emotions without subjectivity getting in the way. In the late 1990s, neuroscientist Jaak Panksepp discovered the precise neuron-to-neuron trail of the seven networks of emotion in the brain: seeking, rage, fear, lust, care, panic/grief, and play.

Panksepp hypothesizes that, by studying and understanding emotions at the neural level, we can understand not only emotions themselves, but also emotional disorders. He believes emotions have similar functions across species, from people to animals. For millions of years, these feelings have helped animals find food, fight off enemies, avoid predators, reproduce, and engage with others. He somehow turned affective neuroscience into a real field when he answered the longstanding question of whether animals have feelings.

For Aristotle, "Man is by nature a social animal; an individual who is unsocial naturally and not accidentally is either beneath our notice or more than human. Society is something that precedes the individual. Anyone who either cannot lead the common life or is so self-sufficient as not to need to and therefore does not partake of society is either a beast or a god." Hence, for social species—such as humans and animals (gorillas, dolphins, orcas, and wolves) who have extremely advanced social organizations and relationships—expressing feelings is key to their survival.

Since the 1990s, affective sciences have grown exponentially considering that today's technology allows machines to read and interpret human emotion like never before. Over the preceding three decades, the analysis of facial expressions and hand gestures has made significant progress, with it increasingly being used in the business world.

The study of emotions actually began with Sir Charles Bell, a multifaceted Scottish anatomist-surgeon. Bell initiated the scientific investigation of the physical evidence of emotions and stimulated the later work of Charles Darwin on facial expressions. Darwin published *The Expression of the Emotions in Man and Animals*, one of the first scientific texts that used photographic illustrations, to highlight his theory.

Darwin's book focused on genetically determined aspects of behavior. His writings, while sharply contrasting Bell's argument, were an effort to support his previous theory of evolution, where all species develop by natural selection as a result of changes in hereditary physical or behavioral attributes. The book then triggered critical studies on the language of emotions, like those analyzing blind-born individuals—whose surprised or blushing expressions were found to use the same muscles and display similar facial expressions to those who are sighted.

Prior to Darwin's book, the study of the face was of interest primarily to those who claimed they could read personality or intelligence from facial elements. Darwin ignored those features. Instead, he focused on the visible but temporary changes in appearance. He wanted to uncover that the expressions of humans' emotions were equivalent to those in animals, supporting his theory that man and animals had a common ancestor.

Fast forward from Darwin's work, and since the 1990s, researchers have increasingly been studying how to create systems capable of reading our feelings and understanding human-like reactions. Australia has begun using a "world-first" system that uses face, iris, and fingerprint recognition as part of its "Seamless Traveler" program, which aims to replace passports control with biometric scanning. Even though security concerns are still pertinent, such recognition technologies are becoming mainstream. In China, for instance, police officers are using surveillance sunglasses to recognize potential criminals. Another example is the iPhone X—which, for the first time in Apple devices, activates itself just with a biometric face scan instead of using a password switch. In addition, present-day computers can recognize deep patterns in vocal pitch, identify rhythm, and if provided with specific software, scan a conversation between two people. They can also identify gender and determine whether there is anger or happiness in their exchange.

Currently, these procedures are solely confined to computers and are used for creating more interactive and specifically adaptive online experiences based on emotion. Can machines become emotion-detecting devices if they can gather data from facial and micro-expressions, posture, speech, and tone of voice? What about from gestures or even how vigorously we use the keyboard? Absolutely they can. Deep learning algorithms can analyze data and identify a mood, even eventually improve it. Will we be comfortable with the fact that AI-empowered robots will be able to read all our emotions and thoughts, probably faster than humans, and act accordingly?

American psychologist Paul Ekman pioneered the study of emotions and their relation to facial expressions, creating an "atlas of emotions" containing over 10,000 micro face traits and gaining the reputation of having created "the best human lie detector" in the world. He even inspired the American crime drama television series *Lie to Me*.

Micro-movements are subtle facial expressions, lasting only a fraction of a second. They occur when a person either intentionally or unconsciously hides a feeling. Seven observable emotions have universal signals: anger, fear, sadness, disgust, contempt, surprise, and happiness. Ekman's original hypothesis, "that particular facial behaviors are universally associated with particular emotions," has been endorsed by other researchers who often use sets of photographs of faces prepared by Ekman himself, to illustrate their studies and prove their research. Today, the seven "particular emotions" Ekman identified are generally assumed to be the "basic emotions" common to all humans and animals.

Importantly, we transmit more data with our expressions than with words. Our faces are tools of emotional communication. Recently, a few pioneering companies have made tremendous progress in decoding emotional states. One of the leading companies that decoded such information and built it into emotionally responsive machines is Affectiva, the first emotion-measurement technology company that grew out of MIT's Media Lab. Its recognition software has developed a way for computers to perceive and understand human emotions based on facial cues and physiological responses.

Affectiva's Facial Action Coding System is a taxonomy of forty-six facial movements that can be combined in different ways to identify and label emotions. The technology uses a webcam to track a user's smirks, smiles, frowns, and wrinkles to gauge levels of surprise, confusion, or enjoyment. The technology can also measure a person's heart rate by analyzing color changes in the person's face, which pulses each time the heart beats. Today, one of the commercial applications for this emotion-recognition technology is helping brands improve their advertising and marketing messages. But what happens when machines become better and faster than humans at reading emotions and predicting our responses? How do we prevent self-improving AI from manipulating us?

Emotionally intelligent computers won't become a reality anytime soon, but when they do, social robots will be a social game changer. Even if having AI with human-like reactions could transform our relationship with machines, we don't want to become more machine-like. We want to (and should) govern technology—we don't want to be governed by it.

People have longed for artificial human entities since the Greeks—the story of Pygmalion, the sculptor who fell in love with his statues, illustrates the depth and antiquity of this desire—materializing partners exactly how we dream of them. Let's drop the poetry and romanticism of the ancient, though, and consider that old plastic dolls are becoming humanoid sex partners that talk back, flirt, and interact with their owners. How will society be affected by it? What are the ethical, legal, and overall human implications of AI-empowered sex robots?

Realbotix, one of the leading sex-doll manufacturers, is already producing ultra-realistic female androids that can talk, submissively follow orders, and remember the sexual preferences of their owners. Most importantly—and disconcertingly—is they are equipped with different AI personalities, for all tastes. "People have accused us of objectifying women," says the owner, "but it's important that people know that this is no more than a sex toy" and that "we're working on a male version of the robot and [that] we'll eventually have a male and a female platform available."

How significant will the implications of such robots be? Let's consider prostitution, which is a tool for harming and exploiting human beings, powering drug markets, and spreading sexual diseases. Can robotic prostitutes change the sex industry? Could sex-dolls be used mostly for specific sexual therapy or for giving companionship to disabled or older people, without weakening human relationships, as the "makers" advocate, or will there be a severe disruption in our society?

Futurologist Ian Pearson predicts that, by 2030, most people will have some form of virtual sex as casually as they browse porn today. By 2035, the majority of humankind will own sex toys that interact with virtual reality sex. He also believes that robot sex will overtake human-to-human sex by 2050. If these forecasts are accurate, does it mean people will have intimate relationships—and may even fall in love—with their synthetic partners?

These "robostitutes" will look, move, and feel a lot like real humans even if their intelligence will be very limited. Through lovotics—the study of human–robot relationships— researchers are trying to engineer affection, attempting to give robots the ability to transmit love. Sexbots (or rather partnerbots), unequivocally designed to bring sexual satisfaction to humans, could be morally questionable since they're typically intended to mimic human beings, both physically and mentally, and won't complain. They will always be capable of being "on" and ready to talk or play.

The fast advancements of these machines are paired with campaigns arguing they objectify women and perpetuate damaging sexual norms, highlighting that these kinds of robots are potentially harmful and will contribute to inequalities in society. Perhaps the use of sex robots, once AI-empowered, could deteriorate human interaction, weaken communication, diminish respect between partners, reduce intimacy, and ultimately—and perhaps prematurely—speed up the integration of humans and machines, where machines will lead the game.

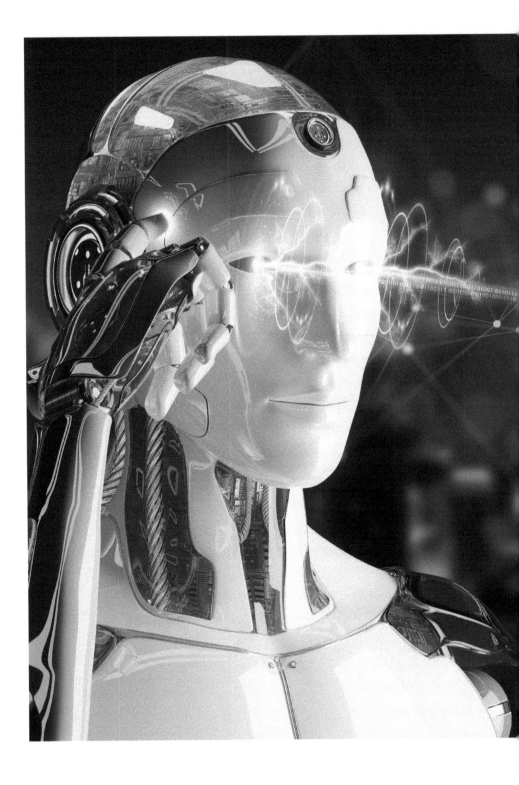

CHAPTER 3:
Uneasy tolerance for machine intelligence

THE TURING TEST: CAN WE REALLY BUILD A CONSCIOUS THINKING MACHINE?

Could "thinking" be replaced by calculation? Could a system understand information from raw data, develop learning capabilities, and apply them as humans do? Children learn by watching, listening, and doing. No one trains infants. They just learn by experiencing their surroundings, and play is one of the leading ways in which children learn. AI behaves in the same way.

A good illustration of this is the first version of AlphaGo from DeepMind, a company acquired by Google in 2014. AlphaGo demonstrated that if a system is fed tens of thousands of data points to analyze, it could develop strategies unknown or inconceivable to humans. It all started by learning from thousands of Go games played by humans, and then the system competed with Leo Sedol, the Go world champion, in a way he thought impossible—Sedol actually initially considered the move a mistake. But it was a brilliant winning move that resulted from super-fast data analysis, a move impossible to be humanly conceived. The computer's digital victory reinvigorated the anxiety of being superseded by machines.

The newer version, AlphaGo Zero, has the capability of not only beating every competitor in the Go game but also learning differently. The system started with a blank, dateless Go board and no data points. The only information it had were the rules of the game, and then it played against itself. After a few hours, the system was able to beat the previous system version by 100 to zero. How did it do it? It did it as humans do, like children do when they start walking. They don't have any rules; they just try until they stand up and go.

It appears, then, that AI systems are slowly venturing outside their pattern of 1s and 0s while starting to learn by practice. This— along with simultaneous discoveries in cybernetics, neurology, and information theory—is increasing the speed of AI development. With AlphaGo Zero scoring an improbable win, we reached levels of proficiency researchers believed we had to wait at least another ten years to see. Indeed, AI research is advancing in different domains—in speech recognition and image classification, genomics, and drug discovery—and in other areas within Google's DeepMind, which has more substantial expectancies than playing games.

In the future, AI could become an essential tool if utilized with a collective approach of multi-systems aimed to benefit society. But what if these systems become unmanageable? Not so long ago, a new AI development was able to mimic human behavior and how the brain works to fill in a CAPTCHA, the acronym for "Completely Automated Public Turing test to tell Computers and Humans Apart." CAPTCHAs are systems designed to prevent bots from accessing computing services, challenging website visitors to identify letters and numbers that are distorted and difficult for computers to recognize. Difficult, but not impossible—as the recent AI development could successfully do so. These new improvements imply that text-based authentications are becoming obsolete and that we need automated human-checking techniques that are more robust. But they also tell us something else—AI is making substantial steps in learning human behavior.

How did it start?

After the Second World War, as the computer era began to flourish, the English computer scientist Alan Turing published a paper arguing that machines would eventually become intelligent and suggested a practical test. The test, an "imitation game," would involve computers attempting to fool people by pretending to be human. Turing's "Computing Machinery and Intelligence" paper was significant because it sought to redefine contemporary themes in artificial intelligence and the ethics of robotics. Besides cracking German Enigma code, allowing Allied Forces to intercept encrypted Nazi messages, Turing initiated a way of thinking about mathematical notions that led to today's AI.

The same laid-out foundations have become an essential notion in the philosophy of artificial intelligence. "I propose to consider the question," wrote Turing, "Can machines think?" Turing's suggestion highlighted how a human interrogator (using the Turing test) could judge natural language textual conversations between a human and a machine, which was meant to generate human-like responses. If a computer is mistaken for a human more than 30% of the time during a series of five-minute keyboard conversations, it passes the Turing test.

In wondering whether a machine could be intelligent, Turing referred to a Victorian-esque competition called the "imitation game," which is set in a parlor and involves a man and a woman, both trying to convince others they are both female. They are asked questions, and an impartial speaker reads the answers. Both have to be convincing about their femininity—something that's natural for the woman but sometimes difficult for the man.

Turing suggested the imitation game could be used as a test to determine whether a machine could think. His version of the game involves replacing one player with a computer—the objective is to convince everyone that both participants are human and therefore intelligent. He thought that AI would pass the test before the end of the twentieth century. Even though we are not yet there, his work started the journey toward achieving human brain replication and eventually building intelligent, sentient agents.

For the past sixty-five years, countless machines have taken the Turing test, but no system has ever passed it. However, in 2014, software called "Eugene Goostman" was at first thought to have passed the test. Chatbot "Eugene" simulates a 13-year-old boy from Odessa, Ukraine, who speaks broken English and answers questions enthusiastically or incoherently—like any typical 13 year old would. Although able to fool judges 33% of the time, passing the threshold set by Alan Turing in 1950, it was later determined that Eugene did not pass the test.

A chatbot is not a supercomputer or an intelligent agent. Computers *can* calculate—but calculating is not the same as thinking.

AlphaGo can estimate moves at an incredible speed, but it does not feel pain. It has no beliefs or desires. More important than everything it can do, it's not capable of producing thoughts. That means it's not a conscious entity. At least for now.

One of the most common misunderstandings about AI is that, once the Turing test is passed, we will have intelligent machines. Will the Turing test ultimately be beneficial in defining convincing reactions within the subjective experience? Unquestionably yes. But one of the defining aspects of these future machines will be their ability to be convincingly human even when it will be evident that they are not human.

In other words, AI won't necessarily be a humanlike intelligence. If we make it similar to us, we will probably weaken Kurzweil's benefits of defeating diseases, compensating for disabilities, enhancing our mental well-being, and providing high-quality education, to name a few. Considering that a superintelligence may become more powerful than humans, we should develop, as Bostrom suggest, AI in a way that makes it human friendly"—in the best possible interpretation of that term.

MINDFUL MACHINES: DO WE FEAR THE BRAINPOWER OF SYNTHETIC AGENTS?

Einstein said, "The true sign of intelligence is not knowledge but imagination." But what is intelligence? Is it the ability to learn from experience, familiarize yourself with the environment, or comprehend new inputs and apply them to their reality? Is intelligence self-awareness? These are important questions, to be sure. But the most significant question is, why do we want to recreate it?

For example, we long to reach immortality or defeat aging. An altruistic superintelligence might analyze and intervene in human genetic codes to help us obtain immortality. It could make humankind omniscient and infallible through trillions of sensors that gather data everywhere: connected wearables, autonomous cars, satellite systems, drones, cameras, smart lenses, and so on. With such assistance, we could become more powerful, evergreen, beautiful beings, forever connected to all the knowledge in the world. And then? What about dreaming, desiring, or **getting emotional?**

Marvin Minsky defined artificial intelligence as the science of making machines do things that would require intelligence if done by men. Yet neither in philosophy nor psychology can we find a standard definition of intelligence.

In 1983, the American psychologist Howard Gardener classified nine types of intelligence: naturalist (nature smart), musical (sound smart), logical-mathematical (number/reasoning smart), existential (life smart), interpersonal (people smart), bodily-kinesthetic (body smart), and linguistic (word smart). While neuroscientists, engineers, and biologists are trying to reverse engineer the brain for speculating from its design, we still lack a solid understanding of intelligence. Nevertheless, we want to create an artificial one.

The field of AI was founded at a conference on the campus of Dartmouth College in the summer of 1956. The attendees—including John McCarthy, Marvin Minsky, Allen Newell, Arthur Samuel, and Herbert Simon—became the leaders of AI research for many decades. It was unthinkable, but they managed to write programs that were, at that time, simply astounding—they built machines that could speak English, win at games like checkers, solve algebraic word problems, and verify logical theorems.

In the '60s, most AI research was funded by the U.S. Department of Defense, and this endeavor helped establish laboratories around the world. AI's founders were extremely optimistic about the future of their discipline, almost certain the problem of creating "artificial intelligence" would be nearly solved in the generation after theirs—believing that, soon, machines would be able to do any work a man could do. However, they underestimated the difficulty of some of the problems they faced, and in the mid-1970s, both the American and British governments cut off all undirected exploratory AI research. Going forward, AI suffered some ups and downs in popularity and funding, which slowed its development.

At this point, robots have largely replaced people in manual labor positions and can perform routine tasks, can acquire information about their environments, and are given autonomy for periods of time. Examples of these systems range from robot vacuum cleaners to autonomous flying drones, acting without human operation and preventing themselves from creating situations harmful to people or the environment. But importantly, they are not self-sufficient. They are not yet artificially intelligent robots, which is the synergy of robotics and AI. They can adapt to different contexts or have autonomous reactions to pre-considered settings, but they cannot adapt to all situations.

Whether safe autonomous systems could be developed was questioned in 2015 after an autonomous working robot killed a 22-year-old German worker who was setting a robot that grabbed and crushed him against a metal plate. There are indications that it was a human error that killed the worker, and even if robot-related deaths are incredibly rare—industrial robots have caused at least 33 deaths over the past 30 years, according to *The New York Times*—this loss has raised concerns more than other deaths.

However, instead of letting ourselves be consumed by fear or denial, since most of what we know about robots comes from popular culture, we should build awareness and show how robots can—and will—change our lives, our work, and our relationships in the near future. We should seek to question their makers on how to build systems that are safe to be near or interact with. Why? These agents will be soon be AI empowered, and we should already foresee on how to deal with them.

The first commercial success of artificial intelligence occurred in the early 1980s when an AI program called "expert systems" could emulate the decision-making ability of a human expert. By 1985, the value of the AI market was over a billion dollars. In the 1980s, AI researchers began to think their software needed a physical body, a frame allowing it to be present in the real world, to be truly intelligent. This hypothesis encouraged an entirely new approach, which led to the assumption that embodying artificial intelligence improves cognition. AI had reawakened the never-ending debate about the body–mind dilemma.

Is there a relationship between the state of thoughts, emotions, pains, pleasures, and beliefs and the physical state of atoms, neurons, and matter? Are sensations and feelings occurring in the mind, or are they happening as a corporeal process? Will unembodied AI be emotionally stunted?

This assumption of being unable to experience the gamut of human emotions raises an important question. Will robots ever feel pain? Ideally, although our brain is analog, we can digitally re-enact almost any neural process. We don't yet have the computational power, but systems today, provided with the right sensor technology, could easily see, hear, and feel the texture and the shape of an object or feel whether there's heat or a lack thereof. They could identify smells, and they could even eventually feel pleasure and pain. They won't, however, have physical experiences like tasting food or feeling sleepy. They will never get drunk or be thirsty, get sick, or feel tired. They will have the knowledge of these things but will not understand the sensations firsthand.

Despite these possibly insurmountable limitations, AI has continued to advance. From the '90s on, AI achieved its greatest successes and began to be applied to domains like medical diagnosis, logistics, data mining, and military applications. The successes were due to a few factors:

- A multi-disciplinary approach establishing the creation of new ties between AI and other fields working on similar problems.
- A new commitment by researchers to solid mathematical methods and rigorous scientific standards.
- The exponential growth of the machines' computational power, also labeled as "Moore's law."

In 1965, Intel co-founder Gordon Moore published his now iconic prediction: over the history of computing hardware, the number of transistors in a dense integrated circuit doubles approximately every 18 months. The forecast was specific to semiconductors and, since then, has become synonymous with the law of exponential growth or the accelerating change law in all areas of technological progress.

History shows that technological change is exponential, contrary to the "intuitive" linear interpretation we apply to all our inquiries. If we forecast the progress of the next fifty years, we easily look back, as a marker, to what happened in the past fifty years. The next century, though, as Ray Kurzweil said, will experience something akin to 20,000 years of progress. There's even exponential growth in the rate of exponential growth.

Within a few decades, machine intelligence may become equal to or surpass human intelligence. The implications include the merger of biological and nonbiological systems, whereby cybernetic brain implants will result in hybrid organisms. Immortal "software-based humans" will live in a virtual world where distinguishing between real or virtual, human and artificial, will be difficult—if not pointless.

Most experts still believe we're several decades from achieving human-level AI. Kurzweil is more optimistic and puts the date around

2029. In this framework, even if the time is still far away, we do need to consider revising some ethical codes. If we do not develop any value-based standards for AI, we risk being subdued by AI makers who will define the new morality.

Today, the topic of ethics and artificial intelligence has the predominant role in all emerging technology conferences. Meanwhile, ethical boards are created worldwide, almost every month. Still, the outcome is always the same: create rules for AI and for its makers. We don't hear much on how to teach AI to behave, but we should. AI—we should not forget—learns by experience. In parallel to the Asilomar conference (which gave us exemplary principles of beneficial AI and a set of guidelines for AI research) or to the many ethical boards that tend to rule or manage AI behavior, we should have a sort of parental board on how to accompany AI from its infant state, to being a toddler, and eventually to being a teenager.

The fundamental issue to consider is that—besides creating ethical principles, behavioral manifestos, or AI golden rules—we should approach the issue with a series of whys. Why do we want to create autonomous machines? Why do we want to pursue autonomy? Is it laziness? Laziness translates into powerlessness. The more we delegate to technology, the more we lose our stamina.

AI is a broad concept, and there are different categories determined by its capability: ANI—or artificial narrow intelligence, referred to as "weak AI"—is a program that simply acts by specific rules and cannot outdo them. It is made precisely to focus on only one task. An example of ANI is the virtual assistant that sits in the smartphone, the tablet, or the computer. The system uses voice inquiries to answer questions and make recommendations. The more it's used and the more it learns and adapts to its user, the more the results become increasingly personalized.

Earlier in 2018 a new Google program, called Duplex, raised several ethical considerations and was a major reflection of the risk this kind of personal assistant could pose. Duplex is a system that can make a voice call to schedule an appointment or a reservation. Even if Duplex is the logical evolution of Amy Ingram—an AI personal assistant able to manage an agenda, arrange meetings, and produce professional and polite answers—it tries to fake being human. Even if it introduces itself as a Google assistant and alerts at the end of the call that the conversation has been recorded, it mimics *ums* and *ahs,* and pauses in an **alarmingly** similar way to an efficient assistant. In essence, it pretends to conduct the conversation as a human being. Again, laziness is impending. Will we be able to make good and fair use of all the time technology is awarding us?

Since the first computers, scientists have assesses the calculating abilities of machines in order to compare them to human brains, often using chess games for testing. In 1997, the legendary chess champion Garry Kasparov was challenged by an IBM computer called Deep Blue. The match lasted several days and received massive international media coverage. The IBMers knew their system could draw from up to 200 million possible chess moves per second, although they were not sure it would win.

Kasparov secured the first game; Deep Blue won the next. The three that followed were all draws. The sixth encounter was a crushing defeat for the great chess master—a victory considered a symbol of AI's promise. It made many people believe artificial intelligence was starting to challenge human intelligence. Today, even a simple chess app can beat human champions.

IBM re-challenged human acumen in 2011 with a new AI named Watson. Again, in front of millions of TV viewers, the system played a game—this time Jeopardy, a well-known American quiz game, and beat two of the most successful human players in history.

The technology in Watson represented substantial progress from Deep Blue. While the chess winner was a supercomputer with a powerful computational outcome that drew on statistics and probabilities for building a game strategy, Watson uses natural language processing (NLP). NLP is an area of computer science and artificial intelligence focused on designing computer programs that understand ordinary speech, grammar, and context; comprehend complex questions; and present the best answers based on supporting evidence and the quality of information available.

Deep Blue didn't actually play chess autonomously. Programmers manually inserted into its memory every single move and countermove. Its cleverness was "speed" in analyzing and building the next step. Watson, as well, was not an independent robot, pushing the button before the others could give an answer. Instead, it was an incredibly fast machine that could find the right answers in the massive amounts of information uploaded into its memory months before the competition.

Clearly, IBMers knew Deep Blue and Watson could not compete with humans—not even with a toddler when it came to the most basic types of human behavior. Although the new developments of AlphaGo Zero made us concerned about the fact that AI is fast improving, we should not fear ANI agents as they are now. They are the primary form of artificial intelligence, and while they can perceive their environment directly, they don't have any concept of the world at large. For example, Google Translate is one of the most extensive ANI systems, as is Facebook Newsfeed. Many of us use both every day, without knowing or fearing AI implications. They focus only on one task. They're good at what they're supposed to do, but they're not a threat. They are just a utility—one that we cannot do without anymore.

Yet the technology is still in the making, and we are not sure whether we will be able to develop a true artificially intelligent system, an AGI or artificial general intelligence, sometimes referred to "human-level AI." While weak, narrow AI is, at best, a simulation of a cognitive process, it is not a cognitive process. Therefore, it is not comparable to a brain or even to part of one. "General AI," though, is a system that should be programmed to genuinely be a brain, with mental faculties like thinking, recognizing, understanding, feeling, solving problems, and above all else, being self-aware.

Basically, general AI would be an agent that is as smart as a human across the board—a machine that can execute any intellectual task we can do. While AGI is still in its infancy, there are some cost-benefit considerations relating to whether the development of it ought to be accelerated or slowed. The setting up of initial conditions—in particular, the selection of a top-level goal for this system—is of the utmost importance. Why? Besides the fact that, for the first time, we should learn how to relate to an entity that is alive but different, it could easily lead to ASI (artificial superintelligence). And it is this that worries scientists and philosophers who are advocating that our entire future may hinge on how we act now.

The AI revolution is the journey from ANI to AGI to ASI, a road we may or may not survive, but one that, either way, will change everything. Since superintelligence may become unstoppably powerful because of its intellectual superiority and the technologies it could develop without approval or assistance, it is crucial that it be provided with human-friendly motivations or endowed with philanthropic, humanitarian values.

Nowadays, advances in technology mean that human beings can allow the mind and body to interact with one another without the need for physicists or philosophers to postulate that the pineal gland or any other component of the human anatomy are responsible for this interaction. For example, doctors have created a brain implant that can power a mechanized arm. It picks up the signals from the user's brain, decodes them, sends them to a computer via a cable, and then allows the user to move the arm, giving back the patient some autonomy.

Another achievement is a mind-controlled prosthetic arm that is dramatically changing the lives of amputees. This time the robotic arm is connected with an implant, which is surgically inserted directly into the remaining part of the bone. A specific surgery performed on the nervous system connects it to the brain, which can command the movements. The amputee is free—both to think and to move the prosthetic limb.

These procedures are still in their infancies, but if we fast forward, now that we also know how to create a substitute for human skin—the one that today is dramatically saving the lives of severely burned patients—could the same technology, in the future, cover an artificial arm or leg and make it seamless? Even hide the fact that it's prosthetic?

Similarly, can we drive AI in a way that will make it useful and friendly? Can we make sure it shares desirable ends and appropriate means with its makers?

Advances in technology have also resulted in new ways of viewing the mind. Marvin Minsky has stated the brain is essentially a computer made out of meat. He has pointed out that both machinery and the human brain are composed of atoms. This means that, when people figure out how the human brain works, they should be able to engineer synthetic re-creations.

Minsky has suggested such technology could enable specific human minds to be duplicated. This suggests that the mind is not restricted to a specific body and is an entity in its own right. The notion that a mind can be preserved after the body with which it is associated dies is an idea supported by cryogenics, a procedure that recently made it possible to bring a frozen rabbit brain back to near-perfect condition.

Although current cryopreservation methods are still unsafe and could cause dehydration and the destruction of neural connections, the rabbit brain experiment was a significant success because it suggests that all neural components, such as memory and personality, could one day be saved for revival. So far, nearly 350 bodies are stored in liquid nitrogen and cryopreserved, awaiting a better time when we will be able to defeat aging and illnesses and eventually achieve immortality. At such a point, theoretically, the corpses would be unfrozen and reanimated. While cryogenics is still not viable to preserve full bodies, today we do have clinical advances in storing sperm and egg cells. But even if we were able to freeze and cryopreserve pigs and human tissues, and successfully rewarm them without causing any deterioration, trying to bring back to life the entire human circulatory system and, crucially, the brain without causing any damage is still an unreachable procedure. Even then, if we are able to bring back to life a body and the brain safely, what about the mind? Will it be frozen, too?

Arguably, Minsky's thinking on this matter views the mind as merely being some form of internal processing unit as opposed to the complex system that human beings have for developing thought processes. However, the nature of the mind is something that cannot be precisely defined. The mind does not require a human body. If it does indeed define whether something is a being in its own right with its own spirit, then this indicates that mechanized creations might one day be truly capable of consciousness.

Minsky stated that, if a sentient robotic machine was asked what kind of being it was, it would inspect itself and state that it appeared to be an agent with two parts: a body and a mind. Unless the robot had learned a theory about artificial intelligence that taught it otherwise, it would put forward the notion that there was some form of separation between its body and its internal process for considering its body and the rest of the world in which it existed. The idea that minds can be created brings up a range of different ethical dilemmas. It indicates that human beings can bring life into other human beings. Some might hold the view that this is playing God. Concretely, though, it means that scientists have an ethical responsibility to the life forms they are struggling to create.

BEYOND THE PINEAL GLAND: CAN OR WILL TECHNOLOGY HAVE A SOUL?

The soul, in many philosophical and mythological traditions, is the essence of a living thing. It is the incorporeal aspect that defines individuality. In theology, since prehistory, humankind had the necessity of recognizing some intangible human substance that was separated by the matter of the body.

The Egyptians, for example, believed the soul has five parts—Ren, Ib, Ba, Sheut, and Ka.

"Ren" stands for your given name and the possibility to be called and remembered, while "Ib" stands for the heart, which holds emotions and thoughts. "Ba" is considered the individual spirit, the personality, and "Sheut" is the shadow, the doppelganger, the other you. The life force, the vital essence that determines life and death, is "Ka."

For the early Hebrews, the soul is identified by three words: nefesh, ruach, and neshama. The "nefesh" is the spiritual existence that resides in the body and is often used to mean "person" or "living being." "Ruach" means "breath" or "wind" and conveys the idea of life as well, while "neshama" is the spiritual existence and the most elevated and purest aspect of the soul. In Hinduism, "atman" means "eternal self," which is the real self, which distances itself from the false self, the ego. Atman, in Sanskrit, means the "self" or "breath," the essence of our existence, while in early Buddhism, a permanent, unchanging atman refers to an absolute and not to a personal self.

The Christian concepts of a body–soul diversity originated with the ancient Greeks, where the soul was considered as at risk in battle and, at time of death, departed to the underworld or the afterlife. The Chinese also differentiate between the ethereal soul, "Hun," which halts with death, and "Po," which stays with the dead body up to decay. Seemingly, then, every civilization has had to analyze and decide about the imperceptible "stuff" we call spirit.

The debate became significant with the advent of René Descartes's mind/body challenge and his denial of animal consciousness. According to him, without the mind—or soul—human beings are fundamentally bodies or mechanical entities, which cannot reason or feel pain, that might act as if they are conscious, but really are not. Because of this, he considers all living things, apart from human beings, automata.

But flipping that idea, what happens when AI-empowered robots can reason? Today, AI engineers are working on building an AGI with an awareness based on a model to mimic the physical world. Ben Goertzel suggests an experiment known as the "coffee test" as a potential operational definition for AGI. The test involves having the robotic system go into an average coffee place and figure out how to make coffee, including finding the coffee in the cabinet, identifying the coffee machine, understanding how to use it, and so on. If a robot is able to make the coffee from scratch, we can consider it an AGI agent. But does it have a mind? What *is* the mind? Can we even define what it means? And where is the mind located?

For Marvin Minsky, "the mind is what the brain does," implying that we can scientifically decode the mind if we rely on insights from neuroscience.

Descartes famously identified the tiny pineal gland as the point of contact between the mind and body. He hypothesized that a small organ within the center of the brain, known as the pineal gland, is responsible for the mind's interaction with the body. The logic behind his theory is that there are two of all the other components of the brain and only one pineal gland. Descartes stated that there are two of all the sensory organs—for example, two eyes and two ears— but human beings only experience one thought at a time, which means that there must be a location within the brain in which two sensations unite before entering the mind. He believed that, since there is only one pineal gland, this transition has to take place within this part of the brain.

Let's pretend René Descartes was right when he claimed the pineal gland is the seat of the mind, and therefore the soul. A few years ago, a study at National Taiwan University suggested that people's brain patterns are altered during meditation. With affordable brain scanners, we can now monitor specific color changes around the pineal gland, mainly in silence. Yet there's still a lot we don't know about this little organ.

We know that it has roles in the immune system, in reproduction, and for the majority of people, in the sleep cycle—it also has a sort of celebrity status in the realms of pseudoscience. However, the "deep in the brain" location of the pineal gland, the epiphysis cerebri, has led philosophers throughout history to conclude it possesses special importance.

In the quest for brain replication, then, what is the role of the pineal gland? If Descartes's "seat of the soul" rules our daily and seasonal rhythms, if it governs our sleep-wake cycles, our hormones levels, our physical performance, and our stress levels—where do we position the little gland? And more specifically, could algorithms manage a binary "pineal gland," wherein their machinations function like the hormones of an augmented human being?

An algorithm is a set of rules or a method to perform some mathematical operation to give a pre-determined result. In a sense, algorithms are problem solvers. Our future lives will be managed by algorithms, step-by-step procedures to calculate every output of our lives. We can, for example, create algorithmic books, developed by aggregating online content on a desired topic. We can generate music or produce paintings. We can perform a search in a fragment of the time needed—the outputs are countless. In other words, algorithms are becoming ubiquitous parts of our everyday lives.

Are we going to be ruled by an algorithmic entity that will oversee our behaviors? At the moment, the human brain can continuously reconfigure and adapt to unexpected conditions. Algorithms, on the other hand, to operate efficiently, have to follow a pre-designed framework with all possible programmed chances. They cannot sustain any transformation caused by their own actions. But what if an algorithm is designed to write algorithms and modify its own workings? To what extent will we—or can we—influence the process?

IBM and Google are promising to create machines, quantum computers, that can process information far beyond any supercomputer we can use today. Is this the next step necessary to develop a fully functional AGI? How will quantum computing impact the development of artificial general intelligence?

The first generation of machines was powered by vacuum tubes and used magnetic drums to store data and memory. These early machines, however, consumed lots of electricity and emitted uncontrollable, unwanted heat, which was a severe problem. Then in the mid-1950s, with the so-called Third Industrial Revolution, the transistor replaced these inefficient early components. The transistor invention gave computers the opportunity to become, with each version, increasingly smaller, faster, cheaper, and more productive. Quantum computing, though, isn't about an improved chip or technology. Instead, it's a new approach to processing information. It consists in a machine that behaves exponentially faster and that can run new types of algorithms to process information more inclusively. We don't yet know—since we currently lack the capability to build large-scale quantum computers—for what such machines will be useful. That means we don't yet know their full effectiveness. We can reflect, though, on how the QuAIL (Quantum Artificial Intelligence Lab)—a joint initiative of NASA, Universities Space Research Association, and Google (specifically, Google Research)—might speed up machine learning and the development of intelligent systems.

As computer science advances, will we design progressively sophisticated algorithms to govern complex systems that learn from experience and act in accordance with the concepts of right and wrong? Can we foresee algorithmic support for benevolent AI development, genome editing, human augmentation, and brain cloning? And most importantly, can we benefit from the superpower of quantum computing to conceive a set of algorithms that will help humanity to design an updated ethical guide that will keep pace with emerging technologies?

CHAPTER 4:
The use of technology to influence society

UNNATURAL STOCKS: WHAT ARE THE GREAT EXPECTATIONS FOR THE EVOLUTION OF EVOLUTION?

Superintelligent beings and brain-augmented cyborgs could supersede natural progression. Given that, to speculate on them is crucial to have—insofar as is possible—a clear image of what came before homo sapiens or how we became human.

Commonly, the history of evolution as a concept traces back to Darwin, who was the first to spell out publicly that organisms change over time as a result of natural selection—a mechanism where species, who can adapt to specific environments, give rise to new species and share common ancestors. Darwin's *On the Origin of Species* was a bestseller that shocked the public, and immediate reactions to the book were mixed. Surprisingly, the strongest resistance didn't come from religious views—which could have, had they existed, been coherent since his theory questioned the Biblical seven days of creation. Instead, the greatest resistance actually came from the scientific domain, which first confronted him with different approaches before, eventually, thoroughly accepting him.

The Catholic Church, for instance, did not denounce on Darwin's theory, even if his approach to evolution could be synonymous with atheism. The Church avoided giving condemnations, although both the scientific and religious communities were already challenged by similar existing theories from Jean-Baptiste Lamarck and even Darwin's grandfather, Erasmus, who was one of the leading intellectuals of eighteenth-century England. He played a key role in transforming British manufacturing and its embrace of innovations and the newly discovered steam power. He also invented windmills, carriages, and other mechanical devices. Most importantly, he asserted that animals evolved from more straightforward, elementary forms.

After a century of seamless disinterest and noninterference in Darwin's theory, the Roman Catholic Church and Pope Pius XII, then at its helm, took a stand with his papal encyclical, *Humani Generis*, which confronted, explicitly for the first time, the concept of natural selection. The Pope stated that there weren't any conflictual positions between Christianity and the evolution theory, expressed by Charles Darwin, as long as they left a space for a divine creator who initiated the process in the time before the Big Bang. A few years ago, Pope Francis reinforced the Church's position, stating that "we risk imagining that God was a magician, with such a magic wand as to be able to do everything" when we think of how life began. He argued, "God is not a demiurge or a magician, but the Creator who gives being to all entities."

Darwin was not alone in researching and speculating on evolution. Alfred Russel Wallace, another British naturalist and today recognized as co-discoverer of the theory, reached the same conclusions—and probably before Darwin. Eventually, in 1858, it was arranged that both scientists would get credit with a joint paper presented at the forthcoming meeting of the Linnaean Society of London. Their work was accepted, but it didn't create a notable, immediate reaction. **Even if scientists of the time knew that evolution occurred, they didn't know** *how*. **Biology forever changed the way we observe and study how we progress and evolve.**

Both Wallace and Darwin admitted that they were inspired by Thomas Malthus's 1798 *An Essay on the Principle of Population*. In it, Malthus proposed the hypothesis that human populations grow exponentially, therefore doubling each cycle, while food supply grows at a linear rate, concluding that **progress of humankind is impossible without imposing limits on reproduction.** Both Darwin and Wallace arrived at the same assumption of **how natural selection leads to evolution and a variety of species.** Darwin, however, was more influential and a better promoter of himself and the theory. He also had twenty years or so of evidence, while Wallace, whose ship caught fire and sunk while returning from an expedition, lost all his specimens and most of his notes.

After their joint publication, the following years Darwin published *On the Origin of Species*, which became the landmark of scientific discoveries. He alone gained global recognition for his position because of his extensive assortment of evidence, while Wallace was supported almost only by the brilliant idea and the few journals he had managed to save.

Evolution as a word has changed its meaning over the years as the concept itself has undergone an evolution. Today, besides biological evolution, we use it for almost everything. It expresses a graphical linear change that we can apply to language, society, politics, and law—and eventually, it should also be applied to ethics.

We further use the Darwinian concept of evolution when referring to culture, where a human cultural change is an evolutionary process, similar to a biological mutation—but a progression of popular beliefs, of knowledge, of customs, and of know-how. It refers to the notion that authority figures, peers, and other non-genetic sources can contribute to adaptive alterations within populations, hinting that cultural shifts could drive adaptations within societies.

Today, the term "evolution" is used in current discussions to refer to the change of species over time, but prior to the 1850s, it was often used to refer to the way in which individual embryos developed. In Ancient Greece and the Middle Ages, for example, it was used to describe a natural state in which everything has a purpose or order.

Even pre-Socratic Greek philosophers started to investigate the early origins of modern evolutionary concepts. For example, Thales stated that life originated in water, hinting that humankind evolved from fish. Anaximander, adding to Thales's theory, asserted that life first rose from the mud and that plants and fish were the only elements in existence; then the fish migrated onto the land, and their fins adapted to their new environment and became legs. They continued to adapt and change until they eventually became human beings.

All pre-Socratics were soundly looking for the same component: the one that acted as a common denominator in all elements—water for Thales, air for Anaximenes. Anaximenes defined the concept of the element of everything—infinite, eternal, indestructible, and in continuous motion—what he called "apeiron." It was Anaximenes, in fact, who laid out the notion of the primordial mass. Although we don't have any facts to support this, he could have even been early inspiration for and a precursor of Darwin's theory.

Who seems to have really influenced Darwin's thought is Empedocles, who is frequently referred to as "the father of evolutionary naturalism." To some extent, Empedocles gave us the earliest mechanism to approach the origin of the species. He believed that all living things gradually evolved via animal parts, recombining to form new entities. Most importantly, he held that evolution occurred via natural selection, with the fittest species possessing a higher likelihood of surviving long enough to pass their characteristics on to the next generation.

From St. Augustine, who expressed the belief that all life forms had undergone a slow transformation to reach their current states, to Leonardo Da Vinci, who stated that apes are close relatives of human beings and noted their similar anatomy, evolution has been a subject of research and controversy.

Lamarck, notably, was the first who openly proposed that organisms undergo evolution, stating that species adapt to their environments to survive. He hypothesized that, when a creature utilized one part of its body to a greater extent than it had previously, this part of the body would change. He gave the example of a giraffe's neck, which had to mutate to adapt to a possible shortage of food, causing a lengthening of the legs and neck. Lamarck's theory was eventually contradicted because his approach didn't have a genetic basis.

In the post-Darwinian era, the concept of evolution was used as the basis for a plethora of different ideological and political standpoints. Many Victorians recognized a world that fitted their social experiences within Darwin's work. The notion that life forms were struggling to merely exist resonated with the public in an era of extreme wealth, poverty, and capitalism. Not surprisingly, this induced some obnoxious theories, such as eugenics, which was used, to some extent, to allow the weak to struggle without offering any aid to them.

After Darwin, various scientists built upon his work. For example, Gregor Mendel identified the way parents passed traits down to their offspring by conducting genetic experiments on pea plants. American scientist Lynn Margulis, who demonstrated that species are capable of evolving via collaboration, further built upon Darwin's theory.

In 1953, some solid evidence supported Darwin's theory as the research of biologist James Watson and physicist Francis Crick successfully managed to decode DNA. They then identified the genes responsible for a shift in color that transformed one variety of mice into another.

Since the early '70s, biologists Grant and Grant (Peter and Rosemary) witnessed evolution in action. They observed that only finches with larger beaks within a specific population could crack the harder seeds that they needed to eat to survive when other food supplies were scarce. We could argue that finches with this characteristic were eventually the sole survivors.

However, not all of the post-Darwinian research backed up his assertions. Darwin's theory held that change is required for evolution to take place, but evolutionary biologist Richard E. Lenski managed to disprove this. Every couple of months, Lenski took samples of rapidly multiplying bacteria that were kept in a non-changing environment and froze them to preserve them. He then compared bacteria with their ancestors and revealed that changes had taken place.

A few years ago, author and academic Juan Enriquez proposed that technology will favor an immediate future in which human beings could become an entirely new species. He has labeled this species "homo evolutis," stating that robotics, tissue generation, DNA manipulation, and overall exponential technology will make it possible.

Theoretically, Darwin's natural selection is somehow surpassed by the fact that we are performing a mutation consciously by unnatural selection since we can modify precisely our own biology and every life form. Enriquez, in his book *Evolving Ourselves*, makes us reflect on the fact that intervening in our evolution could be detrimental for future generations.

We can intervene in our evolution. We can speed up the becoming of another species. But this time we have acquired the making power, so why can our choices potentially still lead us into a dystopian future? Why—since we have the means and can do so—do we simply not structure, ethically and socially, the new species we want to create?

NEW EUGENICS: ARE WE DESIGNING BABIES IN THE SEARCH OF PERFECTION?

One of the arguments that must be raised is that technologies are advancing so exponentially that ethics can't keep pace, with the result that we may face a new eugenic agenda. As with livestock or crop seed, "clients" now have choices and can artificially select traits and qualities in their unborn children or enhance them with technologies. There is the possibility that such resolutions will dramatically change the human race, either by the collective decisions of individuals or by governmental regulation and enforcement in the name of improving the populations of the future. The idea of eugenics—to create better human beings—has existed at least since Plato, who suggested selective mating to provide a guardian class.

While eugenic principles have been adopted as far back as Ancient Greece, the modern history of eugenics began in the early twentieth century when Francis Galton, Darwin's half-cousin, tried to apply Charles Darwin's theory of evolution to humans. Galton believed that desirable traits were hereditary and coined his research as "eugenics," from Greek εὐγενής eugenes, meaning "well-born"—which derives from εὖ eu, meaning "good," and γένος genos, meaning "race, stock." Initially, Galton focused on positive eugenics, campaigning for a healthy society and bearing above average children for an upgraded human race.

Eugenics has always been a provocative, intriguing concept and created controversial debates. In the early twentieth century, it started as a principle and spread to many nations, including the United States and most European countries, which its ideas were supported across the political spectrum. Their concept of eugenics for improving the human population was inspired by the agricultural breeding model, for having better crops. Applied to human species, the strategy to favor the strongest traits and to eliminate the weakest ones was prohibiting reproduction.

The eugenics program climaxed during World War II when Nazi Germany established a state policy of racial hygiene based on eugenic principles that led to the Holocaust and the murder of at least 10 million people by the German state. In the decades following World War II, with the institution of human rights, many countries gradually abandoned eugenics policies, although some Western countries, among them Sweden, continued to carry out forced sterilizations for several decades. In Sweden alone, between 1935 and 1976, 60,000 young Swedish women were sterilized. These women were considered mentally defective or otherwise handicapped to a degree, "which makes them incapable of looking after their children," according to a prominent Stockholm newspaper, *Dagens Nyheter.* The program was conceived as part of a policy of "ethnic hygiene" to improve Swedish "racial purity." Young women as young as 15 years old were sterilized without parental consent, just because they were considered unfit and inappropriate for Swedish society.

Eugenics movements were not elitist but rather incorporated into religion and general attitudes and values of the masses. Even the Bible describes the tale of the Amalekites, who were regarded by the Israelites as an unfit and degenerate people who created evil and should be exterminated. The Old Testament advises that this genocide was condoned by God to prevent the Amalekites from infecting other races, such as the Jews, with their unfit, unclean hereditary lines of degeneracy.

By the eighteenth century, the hereditary nature of degeneracy was considered a known scientific fact. Criminality, masturbation, and alcoholism were considered a biological basis of degradation, and sterilization was the only procedure that could prevent future crimes. This eventually evolved into a sociological theory, named social Darwinism, and became popular in late nineteenth-century Europe and the United States. The theory adopted Darwin's natural selection to condone racism, imperialism, and conservative social and economic policies, justifying why governments, charities, and communities should allow natural laws to play out when it came to poverty, disability, and sickness.

It was Cesare Lombroso who first published in 1880, in *Homo delinquens,* the idea of a separate race of humans. In the Lombrosian model, the concept of "atavism"—the recurrence of certain primitive traits that were present in an ancestor but were not present in intermediate generations—is linked to an irreversible process of the hereditary transmission of internal physical characteristics. He considered atavism as being responsible for creating an inferior population—one of criminals, wild men, and apes.

To protect society, Lombroso believed that careful selection could complement and fortify natural selection. He considered criminals as "throwbacks," primitive varieties in the continuum of the development of the species. He determined that "the criminal is not at all a member of the race of knowing humans," Homo sapiens, but represents instead "a throwback to a residual form of an earlier, more primitive race—Homo delinquens." Lombroso, **heavily influenced by a misinterpreted Darwin,** dealt with issues of eugenics by prescribing programs of physical and mental hygiene to educate the recoverable criminals. And for the ones he considered inferior? A life of imprisonment or even the death penalty.

The Homo delinquens race, it was hypothesized, could not escape criminal and degenerate genetics. Elisha Harris was a doctor who, in 1874, conducted a genealogical study of New York prison inmates, finding that many criminals were the progeny of "Margaret, mother of criminals." Harris's investigation fostered the idea of the "bad woman" who, through promiscuity and lack of class, passes on the degenerate traits to sons—traits that manifest as criminality. These studies, funded by philanthropic eugenists, were critical to supporting social control of the so-called bad women and the sterilization of criminals.

Beginning in 1899, an Indiana prison doctor, Harry Clay Sharp, took a proactive stance of sterilizing prisoners by vasectomy. By 1907, compulsory sterilization of degenerates had become law in the state. In 1927, the United States Supreme Court upheld such mandatory sterilization laws in a judicial case, the so-called *Buck v. Bell*, where 17-year-old **Carrie Buck** of Charlottesville was used to verify the law's legality. Carrie Buck's was sterilized after giving birth to an illegitimate girl and then placed in the Virginia Colony Asylum, the place where the epileptic and feebleminded were confined. Carrie's mother was in the Asylum as well, which justified Carrie's sterilization since, it was argued, the young woman surely shared the hereditary traits of feeblemindedness and sexual promiscuity of her mother. Therefore, it should be imperative not to pass the same characteristics to possible descendants. *Buck v. Bell* is dreadfully known for the quote of one of the most famous members of the Supreme Judicial Court of Massachusetts at that time, Oliver Wendell Holmes. He wrote that "three generations of imbeciles is enough," implying that the court, therefore the government, had the judicial power to decide who can be proactive in the continuation of the species or who must be only a spectator.

The idea that some hereditary profiles are superior to others persists, but what makes a difference today is the sophistication and technology with which such ideas could be implemented to produce an artificially selected, created, or enhanced new species of humans. Do we need to regulate issues related to eugenics, or will such attempts fail since, after all, what is outlawed or banned in one nation will likely be available in another? This may be true to cloning or some genetic design methodology, but what if the future holds a state-imposed restriction on reproduction or even a ban on existence based on genetic weaknesses?

Sociologists Joanna M. Badagliacco and Carey D. Ruiz state that, despite the health advantages that genetic screening and medicine can provide, they are already in use as a means of maintaining inequality. They quote the situation of impoverished Appalachian women working in mines who face prejudice in the eyes of medical professionals as inbred and physically and mentally deficient. These women face reproductive prejudice and encouragement to take birth control and undergo tubal ligation. Why? The authors propose that this is not only a cliché but is true of many women who live in similar poor and rural communities. Compulsory sterilization of populations considered inferior is not new and is still happening. California banned coercive sterilization only in 2014, for example, when it went public that nearly 150 female inmates were "treated" between 2006 and 2010 by the California Department of Corrections and Rehabilitation, who employed doctors to perform tubal ligations. Sometimes without the consent of the inmate.

What happens when human reproductive decisions are made on the basis of social cost? That would be dependent on who is making the decisions, and while the current debate is about the rights of parents to make such decisions, in the future, the fate of hereditary factors and reproduction may be determined by the state or other external authorities.

Potential parents have a considerable choice even without the possibility of creating "designer babies." They already have access to some forms of artificial selection with genetic counseling, prenatal genetic screening, and abortion. The first designer baby, Adam Nash, was born in 2000, having undergone preimplantation genetic diagnosis (PGD) to ensure that he did not suffer from the same Fanconi anemia as his six-year-old sister, Molly.

PGD allows couples at risk of transmitting a genetic disease to their children to be sure they won't inherit them. Thanks to PGD, Adam was born free from Fanconi anemia, and even Molly was able to make a full recovery using the stem cells from her brother's umbilical cord. There is no doubt that this technique is worthwhile, although there are concerns about the embryos, which are discarded by genetic testing.

In 2016 doctor Justo Aznar Lucea explored the ethics of the production process for the creation of designer babies and questioned the commodification of the child, morally questionable gender selection, and the ethics of destroying (is it killing?) the unused embryos created in the process. Aznar's research stated that the creation of Adam Nash required thirty-two unused embryos, and reproductive clinics that specialize in the procedure destroy 98.85% of the human embryos created.

In general, this does not appear to be raising debate outside of technical and academic specialists. Surveys with regard to so-called "designer babies" conducted in the UK and the U.S. reveal that, while there is widespread condemnation of the use of screening for sex selection, avoidance of genetic disease is, for the most part, supported.

Is the use of gene therapy any different from any other treatment or cure for a disease? Augmentation through reprogenetics is at the heart of this issue. Essentially, augmentation through reprogenetics is the use of reproductive and genetic technologies to privilege genetically modified embryos to advance with human enhancement. Its supporters claim that the new liberal eugenics, based on science and individual consent, differs significantly from the old eugenics—which was unscientific and coercive.

Those advocates assert that it is the parents' moral obligation to produce the best children possible. At this time, when a defective gene in an unborn child is identified, it cannot be repaired. We are, however, inching ever closer to that reality. In 2017, two baby girls were treated with gene-edited procedures to eradicate their leukemia cells and today are well and cured. Today, clinical trials of the therapy are even becoming more accepted in the U.S. and Europe.

For many, including professors and bioethicists Powell and Buchanan, the arguments in support of human enhancement are based on an ethics of consequence that could allow procedures by nearly any means—as long as the desired outcome is achieved. For those who support medical enhancement, the action of selecting and purchasing desired traits in an unborn child can be considered similar to music lessons or sports training, but probably more efficient. Do parents have an ethical duty to ensure that their child is disease free, given such technology? In the future, will those children who have preventable hereditary diseases sue their parents for their failure to practice the due diligence of an ethically required duty of a parent to a potential child?

Should we reflect that we are playing with fire? That the so-called new eugenics, although based on science, continues to pursue the same goal as the old eugenics—meaning the development of a superior individual and the elimination of those considered inferior?

Jürgen Habermas, an influential social and political thinker, addresses the question of whether post-metaphysical philosophy can contribute to the ethics of genetic intervention. He predicts that, as a first step, the general population, political public sphere, and parliament may come to consider pre-implantation genetic diagnosis as morally permitted or legally tolerated if limited to a small number of well-defined cases of severe hereditary diseases.

In a next step, he assumes genetic intervention will be legalized to prevent genetic diseases. This would, in turn, lead to a gray area between negative and positive eugenics. To what extent, though, should we use technology in an effort to create better human beings? Who will control the outcome of this progress? Will countries have to rely on communities of people developing and using future tech to regulate themselves in the absence of new and updated ethical codes?

Reproduction aside, it is becoming impossible to draw a clear line between the manufactured and natural human. Other new technological breakthroughs deserve just as much attention, such as the implantation of technology to enhance, augment, or change existing humans. On July 17, 2018, the Nuffield Council on Bioethics (NCB), an independent UK-based organization that focuses on ethical issues in biology and medicine in general, released a report. Its report stated that the intervention on editing human embryos, sperm, or eggs is "morally permissible" as long as the procedure is safe for the health of the genetically modified baby and doesn't "increase disadvantage, discrimination, or division in society." The possibility that a new dimension of the "human" will emerge—one that is designed not to weed out those embryos that are "unfit" but rather to augment them before, during, or after birth—is becoming a certitude.

Moreover, at any given time, we could be just months away from the "brain chips" of science fiction that prevent an individual from even having the thought of taking an action that rebels against the state or denies its authority. It is difficult to objectively assess the impact of new eugenics on human dignity and autonomy. But we can pretty safely assume that those with power will control it, rather than the individuals impacted by it.

Today, it is possible to cheaply obtain a genetic profile analysis, which provides considerable information about a person's genetics, and eventually authorities could use this information against individuals. Already, there are concerns that affordable genetic profiling by companies such as 23andMe could result in rejection for employment or insurance. We are capable of creating mutant animals in the lab, and gene therapy is applied to a limited number of medical problems. But how can this procedure progress without invading our privacy and and still protect our social status?

As noted earlier, forced sterilization has already occurred in recent history, not only that of criminals but also that of persons with various diseases and conditions, as well as among ethnic groups, such as African Americans and Native Americans. For 70 years, since 1909, California has been the region with the highest number of sterilization procedures for both men and women, who were operated on without their consent.

Should the use of information about genetic heredity be confidential, with privacy enforced by the state? Or does such "protection" begin the slippery slide for government and corporations to use genetic information to make decisions? Once jurisdiction is established, future generations may take a more casual view, particularly if it is reinforced by rhetoric, fear propaganda, and cultural values.

On the one hand, new genetic screening technologies have the potential to create a human race that is more resistant to disease, cancer, and disability. On the flip side, though, it is unlikely that such power will be democratized to the individual when it has the capacity for those in power to establish social control. It can be argued, for example, that the costs of genetic diseases are too high for overtaxed healthcare systems, and individuals with possible hereditary conditions may be sterilized, just like Sharp's prisoners. It could be disgracefully argued that the poor are an unnecessary waste of resources as they contribute little to economic progression. Here, the threat of sterilization might also be an effective tool. Implants, molecular changes, or other technologies may be required by the state in the name of costs savings and safety. Human nature may be mutilated by mutant recombination into creatures of war or submission.

Ultimately, it is unknown what would be lost if humans take nature into their own hands. Also unknown is whether what will be lost will improve the health and welfare of future generations or just limit their freedom and their overall humanness.

THE "MISUSE" OF MILITARY EQUIPMENT: WILL THE FUTURE OF WAR BE ONLY ROBOTIC?

On November 17, 2014, Undersecretary of U.S. Defense Frank Kendall issued a memo to the Defense Science Board that could determine how technological innovation will affect human evolution. Below is an excerpt from the memo.

"...The purpose of this study is to identify the science, engineering, and policy problems that must be solved to permit greater operational use of autonomy across all war-fighting domains. The study will assess opportunities for DoD (Department of Defence) to enhance mission efficiency, shrink life-cycle costs, and reduce loss of life through the use of autonomy."

The military is one of the driving forces behind new innovations. It is no secret that both conflict and the fear of it can act as catalysts for inventiveness and technological development. The remains of weapons and fortifications have even been found that were created during the New Stone Age, indicating that military technology dates back to humankind's primitive beginnings. With the arrival of the Bronze Age, humans learned how to create more specialized and efficient weapons. They also developed better handheld protective devices, and since then, guns, rockets, mines, and bombs have replaced the handheld weapons of old. Today, military technology is increasing in its effectiveness, making the world a far more dangerous place as the years go by—and throwing up a plethora of new ethical issues that need addressing.

Friedrich Kittler, one of the most savant media theorists of this century, who passed away in 2011, argued that human beings are no longer the masters of their technological domain—instead, they are its pawns.

Engineers have created a planet ruled by technology, and there is an unquestioning admiration of technological creations irrespective of the fact that they might not result in genuine social advancement. This fascination with technology stems from the fetishism of inventions that became popular due to their military applications. War fuels numerous types of media, and increasingly, conflicts are fought primarily using data flows and information technology, as opposed to manpower. This makes it impossible to fully understand the media because the dominant media technologies control all cultural understandings and the illusions that stem from them. Such technologies define human beings' understanding of the world in which they exist. Arguably, then, the media is dictating the course of humanity, as opposed to human beings creating media content.

Wars are also responsible for numerous innovations that are stripping humankind of its power and placing it within the hands of machines. Similarly, military technology is removing human beings' ability to steer the development of their own cultural institutions and beliefs. We are a society obsessed with technology for the sake of technology.

The military has always been obsessed with secrecy—it's deeply embedded in war's DNA. We look for increasingly sophisticated means of guaranteeing top-secrecy when conveying information. Secrecy is equal to power. With secrecy, governments can restrict and circulate information with ease, and today, wars are mainly fought digitally, with data.

Cyber warfare and weapons are real threats as we can't define the context of conflicts based on emerging technologies. Besides nuclear, chemical, biological, or other innovative weapons of massacre, we should ponder on an electronic, computerized fights where cyberspace become a serious battlefield. What is cyberwar? We do not yet have a global, legal definition, but a national military strategy of 0s and 1s could disrupt the computer systems of another country and easily become a tool of death or mass destruction.

Even if cyber conflicts can be imagined as apocalyptical autonomous robots exploding on specific targets, digital wars are mainly battles over information, where secrecy and security, and eventually an increasing loss of personal privacy, are the only tools for protection. Being a spy today should include having sensible data knowledge—knowing the difference between a computer virus and a malware and knowing the appropriate use of data encryption or digital cryptography.

Codes and ciphers have been used in warfare for millennia. Around 100 BCE, Roman emperor Julius Caesar used a system known as the "Caesar cipher" to protect the contents of messages of military significance so that they could not be understood if they fell into enemy hands. Over time, Caesar's strategy has been disrupted, but it has maintained the same basic structure of replacing letters with other letters or numbers in a fixed position down the alphabet. Even the Mafia with Bernardo Provenzano, now dead and known as the "boss of bosses" of the Sicilian Mafia, used a variation of the cipher to scramble "sensitive information" in notes for his family or subordinates.

Nowadays, governments have specific cryptology departments and utilize extremely complex encryption for military messages. For example, the Advanced Encryption Standard, which is a complicated algorithm, is used by the U.S. military. Blockchain technology, the world's leading software platform for digital assets, allows for fast, secure, and transparent peer-to-peer transfers of money and intellectual property. Such technology could have an invaluable military utilization.

The real game-changer, though, will be quantum computing, which will be able to decrypt contemporary cryptographic methods, making them outdated and easily accessible. In 2017, Chinese physicists launched the world's first quantum satellite, which for now is used for quantum communications. Experts say it could be far more secure than any existing services. By 2030, China foresees that quantum communications will span multiple countries, allowing an extensive computer network to provide quantum Internet and, therefore, solid data protection. We know that technology is a double-edged sword, yet still, we can't foresee the impact quantum computing will have on encryption.

And then there's fake news. What about fake news? It seems somehow innocent, in the context of war, but fake news can become a dangerous conflict weapon. In the 1980s, Russia started engaging in destabilizing activity, known as *Dezinformatsiya*, which does not mean "disinformation." Instead, Dezinformatsiya is a well-conceived communication strategy to undermine the common substrate of a country and deceive public opinion, like what happened in the 2016 American presidential election when Russia used thousands of both human executors and bot computer programs to spread and amplify disinformation about Hillary Clinton's email controversy.

Dezinformatsiya is weaponry that, with the proliferation of social media, is becoming unbeatable. Arguably, technology offers even more support for this potentially new cyber weapon. For example, we have at our disposal a platform that can modify generic audio clips into lip-synced, realistic videos of any person we want. The creator of this platform, which was outrageously tested with a fake video of President Obama, believes that it could improve video conferencing for meetings or facilitate imaginative encounters with historical figures. It is not so senseless to predict, however, that it can also be used for other malevolent practices, such verbally attacking foreign governments or other dangerous applications.

Marshall McLuhan believed that human beings immerse themselves in media to such an extent that they are unaware of the effect that media has upon them. He felt, though, that technological innovation was still a tool of humanity, with the media being a reflection of the world of humankind. Kittler directly stated that he did not agree with McLuhan's argument of media as extension of human senses; "Media are not pseudopods for extending the human body," says Kittler, "they follow the logic of escalation that leaves us and written history behind it."

For Kittler, the media has already superseded humanity, and it no longer mirrors the values, social norms, and beliefs of its creators. He calls it the "theory of misuse," a theory that implies the contemporary entertainment industry is a misuse of equipment that was initially designed for military purposes—for example, the electronic media that are replacing inherited ideas and redefining the nature of humanity itself.

Morally, we are not considering just innovations that have mutated from military purposes to fulfil other functions. Many weapons that have remained true to their original purpose still have associated ethical dilemmas. Arguably, the use of any form of weaponry can never be 100% morally justifiable. However, some weapons are clearly more capable than others of inflicting damage to the fabric of humanity. Weapons that have been created via genetic engineering provide a good example. Making such weapons within everyone's reach, because genetic engineering is becoming cheap and easy to use, can be alarming.

Humankind is no stranger to biological weaponry, either. As far back as 1500 BCE, the Hittites sent plague victims off into enemy lands to deliberately infect their populations with contagious diseases. Since those days, science has dramatically improved our understanding of pathogens and the way the human immune system deals with them. However, these advances have also favored the making of extremely destructive biological agents that are sometimes being used as weapons.

In 2017, Bill Gates, during a speech at the Munich Security Conference, warned the audience about a bioterrorism pandemic originating on the computer screen of a terrorist intent on using genetic engineering to create a synthetic version of a super contagious and deadly strain of the flu. He suggested we should be preparing now for the possible consequences. That we should define now what could be the strategical tool to avoid a large-scale genocide.

Anthrax could also be one such weapon. This disease is deadly enough when it is in its natural state. However, the USSR introduced a gene into anthrax that changed its immunological characteristics, making existing vaccinations ineffective against it. Even the most hardened warmongers would have to admit that there is something ethically dreadful about creating a custom-made illness that is resistant to currently available vaccines.

Tularaemia is another form of bacteria that has been genetically engineered for use in biological warfare. Although this disease only has a 5% mortality rate, it spreads rapidly and leaves people who are infected bedridden for up to two weeks. Again, Russia is responsible for the creation of a genetically engineered vaccine-resistant version.

Geneticists have also figured out how to genetically engineer the smallpox virus to make it even more deadly. The potential for using this disease in biological warfare has been known ever since the 1700s when Commander Jeffrey Amherst of the British forces distributed blankets that were infected with it to Native American tribesmen in Canada. It has a high rate of mortality associated with it and can be transmitted via air. That means, if it were unleashed, it would wreak havoc upon the population into which it was released.

Given such ever-looming threats, international treaties and declarations alike have condemned the use of biological weaponry. The Geneva Protocol bans bacteriological warfare methods, which are commonly understood to include other biological agents, such as rickettsiae, viruses, and bacteria. In 1967, the U.N. published a report on biological and chemical warfare stating that certain biological weapons have effects that cannot be confined to a specific period or geographical space. This means that they have the potential to have irreversible and grave consequences for both human beings and the natural world. Biological weapons are clearly a form of weaponry that has immense destructive potential, one far beyond that of conventional methods of warfare.

The possibilities for genetic engineering within the military domain do not stop at biological weapons. In 2017, DARPA announced a plan to build genetically engineered "super soldiers" with synthetic blood, bionic boots to augment their ankles and Achilles tendons, pain immunization to eliminate the inflammation that causes pain after an injury, and VR-infrared visors that can manage trajectory-adjustable bullets.

It seems, then, that DARPA would like to provide soldiers with the ability to regenerate limbs that are destroyed in battle. The agency is also working on finding ways to remove soldiers' empathy so that they are capable of killing without experiencing remorse or fear. The theory is that this will make them better fighting machines. Since 2015, it is known that the U.S. government is working on implantable memory chips for soldiers to record their actions, as well as on procedures aiming to cure post-traumatic stress disorder (PTSD). These procedures include erasing the individual memories of disturbing events. Our individuality, though, is built by our memories. Given that, how much "brain data" can we erase and remain the individuals we are? Is it ethical to intervene in our own essence of being human?

The Pentagon's research focuses on creating super soldiers— fighters who won't sleep and who have their brains rewired so that they do not experience the terror of fatigue. DARPA has also conducted experiments aimed at figuring out how to genetically modify soldiers so that they do not require as much food to produce energy. It is worth noting that, in a previous incarnation, DARPA was responsible for bankrolling the creation of the Internet. It's not so far-fetched, then, that it could one day be responsible for a military innovation that affects the world on a similar scale. However, such a change could detrimentally impact—rather than benefit—society.

Notably, the British Academy of Medical Sciences has called for new rules governing some aspects of genetic engineering. Some of these rules relate to the possibility that animals might have human brain cells injected into them that endow them with human consciousness, thoughts, or memories. This could potentially blur the line between what classifies as an animal and what classifies as a human being. It poses interesting questions about moral agency, although late animal behavior research suggests that animals may have moral emotions. In fact, several examples demonstrate animal empathy.

Self-explanatory is a video of a monkey who resuscitates his companion after a train accident—the primate moved its injured companion from the tracks and revived him with light biting, hitting, slapping, and water. To confirm that animals are increasingly achieving a distinct status, in 2014, an Argentinian court recognized that one female orangutan has the right to freedom. Sandra, who has spent all of her life in captivity, was granted the status of "non-human persons," with the court finding that she's deprived of her freedom if she's kept illegally in a zoo. Arguably, if animals are given human consciousness, this dynamic will change, and they should be held accountable for their actions.

The issue of moral agency also applies to many other military innovations that different nations are working on. Robots are already used in warfare. If we develop weapons that have more sophisticated forms of artificial intelligence associated with them, will they be considered accountable for their actions on the battlefield?

Wendell Wallach of the Inter-disciplinary Center for Bioethics at Yale University has proposed a moral agency continuum for all technological innovations—from everyday objects that have no moral agency whatsoever to sentient robots that possess full moral agency. This continuum, then, would take into account the autonomy and the ethical sensitivity of each innovation. According to Wallace, two different methods could be used to ensure that robots behave ethically: a top-down approach, in which moral principles are incorporated into the programming of each robot, and a bottom-down approach, which involves robots being taught moral behavior. However, problems exist with both of these approaches. There could be some flexibility in the interpretation of the principles in the top-down approach that a robot could potentially exploit. The bottom-up approach could have difficulty guiding a robot toward specific ethical goals.

To be considered as autonomous agents, machines should first become sentient and have their own free will. Therefore, robots cannot be held accountable for war actions if they are unable to decide whether to shoot and if they lack the canon of respect for other moral agents.

The U.S. military is already spending large amounts of money on attempting to develop robots capable of determining right from wrong. The Office of Naval Research has awarded, as of 2014, $7.5 million to researchers at Georgetown, Yale, Brown, Rensselaer Polytechnic Institute, and Tufts to develop autonomous robotic systems that can differentiate wrongdoing from acting in an ethically straightforward manner. The idea is that robots equipped with these systems will be utilized in military domains in which the lives of human beings are at stake. Situations of this nature could require complex moral decisions. One question, though, is consequential—how can a moral machine be ethically developed if humans have demonstrated that they are not moral champions?

Clearly, military technology has acted as a forerunner for various forms of mainstream technology. This means that if the military is successful in its goal to create robots that are moral agents, they will likely be used for other purposes at some point in the future. What will happen if robot morality is radically different from human morality?

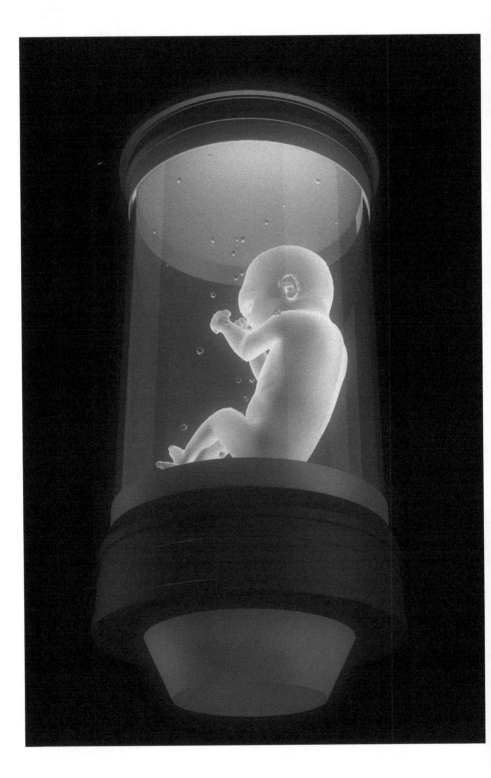

CHAPTER 5:
Artificial means to overcome human limitations

OUT OF CONTROL: IS BIOTECH LEADING INTO NEW POLITICAL TERRITORY?

Historically, social control was mostly an informal and internalized mechanism existing in tribal structures for ruling individuals or group behaviors in an attempt to gain stability and compliance.

Order was necessary to maintain constant survival, and behavior was shaped through the use of traditions, rituals, and the specific morals that formed the foundation of tribal culture. Historically, it's been easier to maintain the continuity and traditionalism of behavior in these smaller societies. With such societies, a blurred line between adequate and inadequate behavior was generally understood and enforced by either inclusion or exclusion from the tribe. The concept of "control" simply referred to society's ability to rule itself. Then, a complex, larger societies had to evolve to develop laws, statutes, and regulations—all enforced by central governments.

Nowadays, as a result of advancing technologies, we will face exceptional times of unusual and diverse crime and terrorism challenges. And the disruptive security implications of robotics, artificial intelligence, social data, virtual reality, and synthetic biology will play a crucial role.

Marc Goodman, a cyberterrorism expert, asserts that technology "is affording exponentially growing power to non-state actors and rogue players, with significant consequences for our common global security." How do we respond to these threats? Innovations could ultimately lead to self-healing computer networks, where crowdsourced knowledge and ideas, supported by AI, could help private and public sectors create systems to identify and annihilate malevolent systems.

In a similar vein, this century will also be remembered for the exponential military technologies that have emerged. As the "gunpowder revolution" modified warfare as a whole forever, cyberwarfare, hypersonic armaments, autonomous drones, AI-empowered robotics, biological weapons, and cognitive science have the power to end civilization. Given that, each new innovation should be well-pondered before being unleashed to the world. Eight nations have successfully detonated nuclear weapons and, therefore, have the ability to end civilization. What does this say about us belonging to the Homo "sapiens" (deriving from the Latin sapi ns, meaning "discern, be capable of discerning") species? One would think such intelligent beings would be smart enough to *discern* that the risk of having a way to end the world is far too great. But alas, perhaps the siren song of amassing "power" makes such discernment an impossibility.

In social science and politics, power is the ability to influence or control the behavior of people. The notion of power can be seen as evil or unjust, but exercising it is a trait that solely belongs to humankind as social beings.

Power is used seemingly by controlling bodies in time and space, yet as individuals, we submit to social control. The practices of disciplinary power subject our physical and biological activities to a system of constant examination and supervision. This, inevitably, allows our behaviors to be regulated—pervasively and continuously. Control over time and space results in control over the operation and position of our own bodies. Why? It fixes where we should be and when. This control maintains the order—just like a component or gear in a machine moves according to its design.

The current rise of technological forms of social control has brought with it a dramatic paradigm shift. Take, for instance, dealing with crime in society. Modern crime technology mostly focuses on crime prevention—surveillance in the form of telephone tapping, interceptions of letters and emails, and electronic monitoring through CCTV camera systems. Collectively, this gives the impression that we're under constant surveillance—forcing us to discipline ourselves. A significant change, however, will happen with 5G networks.

Superficially, gaining another "G" in communication networks doesn't mean that we will have more streaming power. Instead, it means that the Internet of Things—computing devices embedded in everyday objects, that in being connected to the Internet, are able to receive and send data—will increase. With it, the ability to install ubiquitous control devices will increase. While this could certainly make our daily lives easier, it can also undermine our privacy and our health. Recently, in January 2018, the Trump administration had to deny a memo that reported its plans to build ultra-fast networks, obviously as a means of control in the name of safety and security. Even if we do not have the fifth generation of cellular networking in place yet, we should consider the pros and cons of such technology.

As early as 1795, Jeremy Bentham proposed a constant surveillance theory, the "panopticon," which was conceived as a circular building with an inspection tower in the center, from which inmates could be continuously watched and controlled. While inmates are always-on, they can't see through their cells. Bentham conceived this strategy as well for factories, schools, and hospitals— where the people inside would be unable to tell if and when they were being guarded. This would make discipline a relatively passive rather than active action.

Michel Foucault builds on Jeremy Bentham's model of the panoptic prison, considering it as the initial point for showing that this model of power control is actually at work in society at large. In such a prison, Foucault suggests, the ever-visible inmate is always "the object of information, never a subject in communication," labelling the function of discipline as an apparatus of power.

The panopticon metaphor has other far-reaching impacts for surveillance in the digital era. Will we have a panopticon society—a police state characterized by omniscient surveillance and mechanical law enforcement?

The partitioning of the body in space is cellular in that it is partitioned and gives illusions of freedom within a confined space. The prison is divided into prison cells. The school into classrooms. The high-rise into apartments. This is all part of the control of space of which Foucault speaks. The only way to win more freedom is to become the one who keeps that order. The prison guard has little more freedom than the prisoner, and the teacher has only a little more freedom than the student. That small amount of freedom, though, is used to exert further discipline. Foucault argued that such practices were initially nurtured in segregated institutional settings, such as schools, factories, hospitals, military establishments, and prisons. Then, he says, they were applied increasingly more widely until they were the universal methods of social control and regulation.

In this upsetting scenario, millennials act as the game-changer. Unlike the previous generations, they don't count on a predictable life—the same job, the same city, the same domicile. They don't dream of buying a house or starting an ordinary family. They value experience over property or possessions. That means their mindset is disrupting Foucault's notion of confined space.

Foucault reflected the emergence and nature of modernity through a genealogy of daily micro-practices, which he believed to be the basis of modern power. It is such a scenario that forms the bulk of what power is considered in bioethics. It's a power that developed in response to challenges created by the specifics required in the regulation and control over bodies in the post-war period, such as the criteria to define death and the time of death. These criteria had become contentious with the use of life-support systems, organ transplants, and other technologies. This social order of medicine is culturally constructed. And yet despite creating clear distinctions of life and death, taken as fact, they remain no more than a guess. It would be fascinating to know Foucault's positioning in this era of exponential medicine, where every day we gain new knowledge of our bodies.

With disciplinary power, the main objective is to concurrently optimize the body's productivity, skills, and capacities, and cultivate its docility and usefulness. Such power over the body can be seen in the schedules that we keep and the borders that we maintain. Foucault calls it "biopower"—which he defines as "an explosion of numerous and diverse techniques for achieving the subjugations of bodies and the control of populations." Biopower is centered on both the management power of the social body by regulating disease, sickness, death, health, birth, and sexual relations (among others) and the disciplinary power, which is focused on the human body as an object to be monitored, trained, and manipulated. A body under this intrusive power becomes docile.

Using Foucault's ideas of the docile body, health and medicine have been analyzed and critiqued extensively in terms of how the profession controls the way we view our health and what we do about it. Since this medical system is further commoditized as a doctor visit, pharmaceutical products, therapies, and secondary services as quantified self-movement devices, we are in fact paying the health profession to control us and (to control) our perceptions of the health of our bodies.

Foucault is mainly concerned with surveillance and public health. He found mental health and the identification and treatment of mental illness to be particularly about treating the healthy by excluding or removing the ill. The concept of illness in terms of mental health is defined as the one that deviates from the norm, giving to those who hold the authority of decision-making the means of disempowering the mentally hill. Today's technology gives us the impression that we have free will in deciding our health pathway, but that's not always the case.

While AI is transforming and redesigning healthcare, becoming an indispensable medical tool for research and diagnosis, who's going to keep and own the shared data? How can we ensure that AI won't be biased by conditions that were considered illnesses in the past? For example, homosexuality was medically considered a mental illness until late into the twentieth century. Such concepts were no more than social constructions without any basis of the body. However, homosexuality involved behavior that society wished to control. How can we be sure that AI will be free of such biases?

It is not just body processes and health that are controlled, but our bodies themselves—which bodies, where they are, when, and why? The treatment of the Roma population, a typically itinerant ethnic group who lives mostly in Europe or the Americas, provides a clear example of the use of biopolitics to control the undesirable. In this respect, Italy has had a policy of isolating Roma in camps for over three decades. In 2008, the Italian government took things a step further by conducting a massive collection of fingerprints, creating a database of all Roma in Italian camps. This was followed by deportations. Those Roma who remain are either scrutinized in state-run camps far from Italian cities or they become internal exiles. While these practices are justified by immigration laws, other authoritative sources, and some crimes committed by Roma immigrants, the fact remains that the Roma born in Italy are illegally born and have no capacity to rehabilitate their status. They are, essentially, considered unfit for Italian society. Meanwhile, the European Commission is refusing to take action.

Thus, innovations over the modern era, from fingerprinting to retinal scans, have provided those in control with new and more sophisticated biopowers. The result is the convergence of biopolitics and social control in the form of new programs based on technology, such as the Aadhaar biometric identification database in India. India has undertaken the largest biometric identity database in the world and intends to issue a unique identification number (UID) to all 1.3 billion residents with its Aadhaar program. So far, over a billion Indians have enrolled and received their twelve-digit biometric identity number.

This biometrics-based digital identity is assigned for a lifetime, and it is based on fingerprint, iris scan, facial recognition, and biographical data. The program allows citizens a single window to access programs, such as welfare, medical services, and education, as well as personal banking accounts. The biometric sub-system uses multiple-source biometric data points to ensure de-duplication and accurate identification for verification. The justification for the Aadhaar system includes the assurance of unique identity, mobility, and movement; a reduction of fraud; and the provision of services to the poorest, including a reduction of the costs to supply such benefits. Progressively, the private sector—such as insurers, banks, background verification companies, and telcos—is adopting this authentication system, not only to verify identities but also as downloadable customer data archives.

In early 2018, an Indian journalist managed to acquire, over WhatsApp with less than 10 dollars, Aadhaar data from an unidentified seller. This raised global concerns over privacy and data violations because the reporter was able to acquire citizen data and eventually print new ID cards. Thus, elements related to how the data will be used and issues with protection and access, given the lack of legislative guidance, remain of essential importance.

In addition to concerns regarding lack of explicit legislative protection for privacy, the ability to relate all data regarding government transactions and demographic information could be used against individuals, limiting their mobility and freedom. Aadhaar allows for what is essentially a surveillance system. Through government program transaction data, it gives knowledge regarding where individuals are and what they are doing. Very likely, the system will be used in the future to control the large and rapidly growing population of Indians through the subtleties of the system and the information that it provides to decision-makers.

China is also creating an identity database system for developing a national reputation. By 2020, the government will assign every citizen a "social credit score" that will determine people's ranks in society depending on their social behavior. This is an example of how China wants to gain trust nationwide and build a culture of transparency. The system will focus on four domains: honesty in government affairs, commercial integrity, societal integrity, and judicial credibility. Low scores result in punishment, and in its early 2018 rollout, the system has prevented people from taking 11 million flights and 4 million train trips. If the Social Credit System rolls out as promised, it will become a new way of monitoring both the behavior of individuals and of companies. Even today, it has created several controversies because low credit scores can blacklist people, placing them on the margins of society. Low scores can also be assigned for spending too much time on Internet habits like gaming, for failing to conform with court judgments, or for misbehaving in public spaces or on public transportation. Human Rights Watch considers this strategy "chilling." **While the system has encouraged "good" behavior and can make social life easier, it raises serious ethical issues.** Who determines the parameters of "good" and "bad" behavior? Is it the government, the creators of the software, or an ethical board who decides the standards of proper behavior?

These latest technologies developed to promise well-being or a straighter society are not only about training or disciplining the body. Rather, they are also interested in and concerned about where the body—and therefore the individual—is in space and time, and what life activities it is allowed to be engaged in. Genetic engineering presents a further challenge to privacy and autonomy. In the early days of genome mapping, there was concern about the often-touted benefits of genetic mapping. Analyses were based on concepts of normal and abnormal, and of health and disease that were not adequately analyzed or understood in terms of how they would serve to legitimize social control.

Social control requires the control of bodies, definitions of normality, and legitimization of an authority that can regulate and enforce that control. Discipline of the body includes the identification of that which is allowed, that which is criminal, and that which requires "assistance" in the form of hospitalization, quarantine, or isolation. In addition, there is, of course, the hyperbole associated with biotech. The new biology will challenge everything in its pathway, including the understanding of ourselves, our relationship with the world, our social arrangements and values, and our political systems. Are we facing a scenario where the new species that we are almost certainly becoming will be able to self-regulate? Or should we rely on a system of digital ethical codes administered by an invulnerable and unbreachable artificial intelligence?

ECTOGENESIS: ARE WE FACING THE AGE OF MOTHERLESS BIRTHS?

Efforts to mimic nature's reproductive powers are nothing new. Why do we advocate that embryos should be carried by their mothers? One of the reasons is that the connection that is developed during pregnancy creates an innate bonding between the child and the mother while she becomes uniquely protective and attached.

By around twenty weeks old, babies start feeling their mothers' touch, and sometimes they answer back. Unborn babies can also hear the mother's voice before birth, and while this experience is not scientifically proven, the higher levels of oxytocin—the so called hormone of love and bonding—can imply a link that a child feels connected to the mom when in the womb. Crucially, this requires further investigation because it falls within human and animal nature. A fact that becomes hyper-relevant in the content of considering the abolishment of this natural pattern. Could ectogenesis, the development of embryos in an artificial framework, harm the relationship between the child and the mother? Or will it establish an equal exchange, from the start, for both parents?

In 1985, after publishing *Making Babies*, Peter Singer made a bold public statement that endorsed ectogenesis: "I think women will be helped, rather than harmed, by the development of a technology that makes it possible for them to have children without being pregnant," he said. Singer's vision echoed radical feminist Shulamith Firestone who, in 1970 stated that "pregnancy is barbaric." She questioned when the "freeing of women from the tyranny of their reproductive biology" would occur so that they could finally reach full equality with men. Viewed this way, artificial wombs are merely another step in the ongoing advance of human reproductive technologies and women's social equality. They would both expand the range of reproductive choices and make the differences between men and women a matter of technological convention rather than biological nature.

In the past few decades, women's reproductive freedom has conquered significant achievements. Abortion, contraception, and sterilization techniques have allowed women greater control over fertility. While feminists have been unified in support of methods that enable women to control their own fertility, feminists disagree about new reproductive techniques designed to treat infertility and induce pregnancy. Some feel that in vitro fertilization, embryo implants, and research for ectogenesis should not be supporting pregnancies or replacing the act of giving birth. These experiences should instead be granted, as nature intended, to women.

Ectogenesis, or using artificial wombs, is basically the growing of a creature inside an artificial setting outside the body where it would ordinarily be found: for instance, the growth of a fetus outside the body of the mother. The same case can be argued about the growth of bacteria and microorganisms outside the body of the host.

In a historical account, the initial known suggestion for an ecotogenetic procedure comes from the alchemical genius Paracelsus, who straddles the borderline between medieval and modern. His proposal encompasses forming a homunculus by closing up semen within the uterus of a horse and permitting it to become rancid for about forty days on a regimen of human blood. He wrote:

"Let the semen of a man putrefy by itself in a sealed cucurbite with the highest putrefaction of the venter equinus for forty days, or until it begins at last to live, move, and be agitated, which can easily be seen. After this time it will be in some degree like a human being..."

Paracelsus was a Renaissance physician and alchemist who pioneered the use of chemicals and minerals in medicine. Alchemy played a significant role in his activities and overall in the development of early modern science—though it was often referred to as magic.

French chemist and physicist Paul-Jacques Malouin describes "alchemy" as the chemistry of the subtlest kind, which allows one to observe extraordinary chemical operations at a more rapid pace, operations that require a long time for nature to produce. Natural philosophers, such as Vesalius and William Harvey, helped turn alchemy into chemistry. Robert Boyle, one of the most recognized alchemists who possessed one of the greatest creative and insightful minds of the seventeenth century, left a handwritten list (discovered after his death) in which he predicted such things as "the prolongation of life," the "art of flying," and "perpetual light." He also speculated about the possibility of sleeping tablets, artificial stimulants, antidepressants, and drugs to "exalt imagination." Boyle even predicted that we would eventually accelerate the "production of things out of seed" and be able to "transmutate" minerals, animals, and vegetables—all precursors to what today we call nanotechnology, synthetic biology, and genetic engineering.

After Paracelsus, for a long time, there weren't any notable debates on growing life outside women's wombs. The contemporary ectogenesis argument didn't emerge until the 1920s, and since being introduced, it has been labeled with different names—synthetic wombs, artificial uteruses, and uterine replicators.

The term "ectogenesis" was invented in 1924 by British scientist J.B.S. Haldane, who, in his book *Daedalus*, described in detail most of the biological advancement during the twentieth century, outlining the discoveries that put ectogenesis on the path to normality. He claimed that the technology, in which a human fetus can grow entirely out of a mother's body, was ambitious but not unrealistic. To refine and enhance the human race, he argued, abolishing pregnancy could be worthwhile. He predicted that, by 2074, live human births, involving mothers, would make up less than 30% of all births.

Clearly, Haldane was a life-long supporter of eugenic ideals and the use of eugenic plans and controlled reproduction. After it became apparent that the conclusions of the eugenics movement were invalid, however, he slowly turned against the movement, or at least against some of the significant aspects of the mainline eugenics measures. Despite those changing views, he vividly supported artificial wombs until his death.

Over time, numerous documented articles have confronted Haldane's proposals and the significance of his futuristic developments. The most well-known of these initial arguments regarding ectogenesis is neither scientific nor philosophical. Rather, it is a dystopian science fiction book, *Brave New World* by Aldous Huxley (1932), which is becoming less dystopian since many predictions are actually coming true. Contrasting the principles of computerization and mass production initiated by Henry Ford, Huxley portrays a world in which individuals are actually nurtured and grown in different batches according to certain rules designed to create tailor-made beings suitable for specific tasks. Huxley's characters are an unsettling set of inhuman mechanisms, each fabricated to fit a role. Even if this dehumanizing depiction of ectogenesis warned us about the hazards of reproductive experimentations, contemporary biotechnology is progressively advancing to facilitate extra-uterine gestation. Such advancements could improve premature baby survival and solve infertility for good. But should we proceed with this procedure? Who will control it? Is it going to be the doctor, the government, the parents, an international ethical board?

In 1978, we ventured into the first successful process of IVF, a procedure where an egg is inseminated outside the uterus of the mother and then implanted. Fast forward several years later, and in 1993, the U.S. government approved a patent request for an "artificial uterus." The suggested device is a system for life support for a premature baby where the baby continues to be held to its placenta through the use of its umbilical cord. For a precise medical or biological process to be considered as ectogenesis, though, it should allow the fetus to grow without the mother, from fertilization to maturity. Even if partial or limited ectogenesis could help an extremely premature baby to develop, we should reflect on all the pros and cons—and eventually on the ethical issues of a full and established ectogenesis procedure.

Today, the technology is starting to evolve even more. In April 2017, a consortium of international scientists from Japan and Australia was able to use an innovative artificial womb technology to successfully incubate a lamb for a week. They're predicting a similar procedure to help preterm babies to fully develop.

Regardless of the current state of technology—yet especially because of it—ectogenesis ultimately raises substantial social concerns. For instance, what will the impact be on the interests of the potential father and state of the fetus? Who will enforce the contractual agreements concerning artificial wombs? Who would be accountable and liable for the complications, if any, that might take place as a result of the use of ectogenesis?

The mother can no longer claim to have the unique right to control or decide what happens to the embryo. Instead, this procedure could equal the rights of both men and women regarding abortion, considering that the being is gestated by a nonaligned proxy—a surrogate, artificial womb.

A number of supporters consider ectogenesis a beneficial medical advancement since it offers protection and safeguards for the fetus by providing a viable option outside of abortion. Instead, such embryos can be positioned into an ectogenetic incubator and eventually put up for adoption. The process could, then, serve as a middle ground for the pro-lifers who are against abortion and the pro-choicers who believe that they ought to have the right to abort fetuses if they do not want them, allowing the pregnant females to terminate pregnancies without disposing of the embryos.

According to the World Health Organization, one in ten babies are born prematurely. Thus, artificial wombs, if developed only as a medical device, could support difficult or risky human pregnancies. On the contrary, a full-term ectogenic chamber could raise concerns on how to guarantee to the baby born from the surrogate wombs the same legal rights as a baby born from natural pregnancies. There is no doubt that ectogenesis presents several medical benefits, as well as potential threats for this technology to be abused. Therefore, parallel to scientific and technological discoveries, ethical, legal, and social aspects should be addressed and thoroughly discussed now— before the procedure becomes available.

Most importantly, though, we should reflect on the fact that a woman will forever remember the pain—and—joy of giving birth. Why should we give it away to technological advancements? Shouldn't we nurture and protect our core essence of being human?

HUMAN ENGINEERINGS: IS IT PROPER TO INTERFERE WITH NATURE?

Artificial wombs, artificial intelligence, and artificial humans—what does it mean to be human? Do we lose humanity with the use of technology? What is the distinctive element about being human?

For Aristotle, being human means having the capacity to reason—with the ultimate goal being to develop individuals' reasoning powers. When they do this, they are living well, in accordance with their true nature, and they will find the most rewarding existence possible. In Christianity, the biblical notion of humankind serves as the image and likeness of God. In the Renaissance, the concept of "being human" is totally inspired by the idea of human self-sufficiency, of man's boundless abilities.

Descartes worked on the notion cogito, ergo sum—"I think therefore I am," which made reasoning the unique feature of humans. Soul and body were understood dualistically. The body was regarded as a machine, similar to that of the animals, while the soul was identified with consciousness.

Centuries worth of scientific thought, artistic tradition, and spiritual practice have attempted to answer this most fundamental question about our existence. Before anyone considers giving humans greater brainpower, or unnatural birthrights, we should probably first consider the consequences of a life where there will be no distinction, post-singularity, between human and machine.

"The human organism is enormously complex," affirms Bostrom. "If we go in blindly and change things at random, we are likely to mess up."

In humans, as with any other organisms, genetic engineering refers to any DNA manipulation using various technical methods. Nowadays, genetic engineering is intended as "enhancement" to produce a useful or desirable characteristic in an organism on a molecular level. Such procedures may include additions, deletions, or targeted changes to the genome. These alterations can involve the introduction of genetic material from either the same organism or from different types of organisms.

Humans have altered species' genomes for thousands of years through domesticating wild species, by selecting seeds of wild plants for farming, or selectively breeding wild animals. They did it for efficiency—that is, for more productive farming or to increase profit and to secure themselves a better future. Selective breeding has advantages and disadvantages, however. For example, weather crops, if well-bred, can grow more than natural crops. Selectively bred chickens can lay more eggs or cows more milk—this, in turn, can increase production and create stronger plants and animals. But it could also lead to speeding up unnatural, harmful mutations and eventually to the loss of species. While the notion that evolution happens by natural selection is settled matter, defining the best characteristics of the best—the parents—and breeding the next generation is a fascinating but scary process. Shouldn't we be concerned with the consequences of speeding up evolution?

We absolutely should—but technology is sexy. It makes us dream. And thus, we dream that we can achieve everything we are able to envision. The next step could be cloning. In nature we already have plants that clone themselves with asexual reproduction or animal-like starfish and other relatively simple sea creatures that generate offspring that are genetically identical to a single originator.

In the 1950s, frogs were the first animals to undergo cloning, and since then, although reproduction of mammals in the laboratory is relatively new, we did create Dolly, the sheep, in 1996. Thereafter, researchers have been trying to use the cloning technique to produce livestock, such as champion horses or cows that have been replicated in an attempt to allow farmers to better boost their finest animals. This scenario, however, is still unsettled. Food from clones and their offspring, for example, is not yet allowed to enter the food chain because we are still uncertain about the safety of the food these animals can provide.

In China, Boyalife Group, which has stated that it's building the world's largest cloning factory, admits that it already has the technological knowledge to clone humans—but it's not yet in their plans. It has a gene bank that has collected the DNA of 1.38 million people and 960 trillion bytes of DNA data, and it is planning to establish China's most extensive health and pathological specimen cluster. It also wants to become the largest animal-cloning factory—for now, it only holds that title in Chinese territory.

Today, we're starting to accept cloning as an ordinary procedure. We clone our beloved pets as Barbra Streisand did, though it's not cheap. Her dog, Samantha, died, and Streisand had genetic material taken from the dog and she had two puppies cloned. The main issue is that, in order to have her dog truly back, she needed to not only aesthetically clone her dog, but also the temperament, the behavior, the conduct, the style. Eventually, she realized this was impossible since the puppies are different dogs. Streisand's endeavor highlights an important question. Are we inventing, developing, and using all these new technologies because we still cannot accept the thought of death?

Jack Williamson coined the term "genetic engineering" in his science fiction novel *Dragon's Island* in 1951, forecasting James Watson and Francis Crick's DNA discovery—the double-helical structure of DNA. In reality, DNA was identified nearly ninety years earlier by Swiss chemist Friedrich Miescher, who, while studying blood, isolated a previously unknown type of molecule—he called it "nuclein"—concluding that the element was part of the cell nucleus. This paved the way to today's DNA experimentations.

Every cell in our body contains a copy of our genome. That includes over 20,000 genes—three billion letters of DNA. DNA is a complex molecule that encompass all of the information necessary to form an organism. In basic terms, human genetic engineering is a way to manipulate genes to make the human body closer to perfection. Nonetheless, do we know what perfection truly means? If we can codify it, is it really achievable? If achieved, will we be bound by the ethical and social implications?

Genetic engineers used to say that what we needed was a system for altering DNA, similar to how a word processor can correct a simple mistake. With such a tool they could then fix mutations without tampering with the rest of the genome. They could replace one version of a gene with another or insert new sequences precisely where they should go.

After several trials, we currently have a recent procedure known as CRISPR-Cas9, which stands for Clustered Regularly Interspaced

Short Palindromic Repeats. The technology isn't only revolutionary—it's also more efficient, faster, and more accurate than other existing genome-editing techniques. And it is essentially pretty cheap. In 2017, scientists were able, utilizing CRISPR, to extract HIV from a living organism, leading to a probable solution to the infection. This presents promise for preventing muscular dystrophy in mice, attacking cancerous cells, or detecting specific strains of dengue or Zika, among many other applications. Eradicating diseases is surely an incredible advancement, but is it only this aspect we should focus on? CRISPR offers the promise of many more developments.

Beyond ending disease, human genetic engineering also has the potential to prolong the lifespan and, most importantly, help cure illnesses and diseases in unborn children. CRISPR can also facilitate de-extinction, the method for bringing back to life species that have gone extinct. But do we really need to do this? If nature decided to extinct a species, why do we want to revive it? What do we gain from de-extinction technologies? Besides curiosity, extinct species could help us to better study evolution and restore a lost environment. But it could also endanger our current ecosystem with retroviruses and other extinct pathologies. Shouldn't we think twice, then, before focusing on reviving the past? There is a real potential in gene editing, to be sure. We can eliminate major chronic or genetic diseases affecting millions of people. But we should stick to the procedures where we can foresee the potential consequences.

The big challenge is the diversity of regulations that rule the methodology, in particular in allowing human testing and defining the role of the embryo in such experimentation.

Do embryos have human rights? Should they be created and destroyed to allow genetic testing? With CRISPR/Cas9 and other genome-editing technologies, germline modification—which is the genetic procedure that involves changing genes in eggs, sperm, or early embryos—is becoming viable, although it has been off-limits for both safety and ethical reasons. In 2017, though, according to the magazine *Nature*, the U.S. National Academy of Sciences (NAS) and the National Academy of Medicine in Washington, D.C., stated in a report that such a clinical trial "might be permitted, but only following much more research" on the pros and cons, on the risks and benefits, and "only for compelling reasons and under strict oversight." **In other words, we now are starting to have a sort of a green light, even though we have not yet ruled internationally on what is allowed and what is not. Who decides what reasons are considered compelling? Who should decide?**

China seems ahead of this discussion since it has already been using gene-editing technology since 2015, and it appears so far that at least 86 patients have been treated for HIV, leukemia, and cancers of the kidney, lung, liver, throat, and stomach. In 2017, Chinese scientists also published a report that they worked on healthy human embryos, using the CRISPR genome editing technique, and managed to correct genetic mutations in at least some of the cells of three of them. Do the Chinese have different rules? Perhaps. Confucian thinking says that someone becomes a person after birth. Therefore, embryos in China could be regarded as less of a person that what constitutes personhood in the Western world. In order to search for a global ethical resolution for germline intervention, we should tap into social practices and moral principles of each country involved in the research.

Currently, an international ban on performing tests and experiments on human embryos does exist since we have unclear borders on what is possible and what is not. What we know is that, if these tests are performed outwardly, they could lead to irreversible, uncontrollable changes—editing human embryos today means intervening and changing all body cells of the future beings. What cost, if any, will we pay for this epic marriage between computer technology and genetic engineering?

International meetings, public and private convening, debates and discussions are taking place while researchers are increasingly able to perform their research faster, cheaper, and more accurately. We should accept that we have already opened the door to human enhancement. But is there another way to write the rules?

We worry that these technologies might undermine our human essence, our human dignity, or carelessly impair something that is deeply valuable about being human. Yet it is exactly that essence that is difficult to explain since more than 2,500 years of civilization have net yet been able to give us a proper definition.

In some cases, the unease seems to derive from religious or crypto-religious sentiments, whereas for others, it stems from secular grounds. The best approach, bioconservatives argue, is to implement global bans on swathes of promising human enhancement technologies to forestall a slide down a slippery slope toward an ultimately debased posthuman state. Comprehensive bans, however, do not work, and we don't want to slow down progress. Rather, we want to live a healthier life, freer of diseases, but as well, we want to be in line with our moral beliefs of respecting the essence of being human. Who, if not philosophers, could help us respect our own humanness? Should we allow philosophers to sit at the scientific debate table since we are starting to gaze at and ponder our humanness?

CHAPTER 6:
The "reality" of virtual worlds

H+: ARE WE PLAYING GOD?

So far, I've argued that the rapid improvement in core digital technologies is fueling exponential innovation and eliciting ethical alarms. A movement known as "transhumanism" has also come about in recent years, with an eventual goal of fundamentally transforming the human condition by developing and making widely available technologies to greatly enhance human intellectual, physical, and psychological capacities. Fueling the movement is the Humanity Plus organization (formerly known as the World Transhumanist Association), which was funded by Nick Bostrom and David Pearce to advocate for the ethical use of emerging technologies to enhance human capacities.

Transhumanists focus on the potential benefits and dangers of emerging technologies that could not only surpass fundamental human limitations but also transcend the ethical codes of developing and using such technologies. Essentially, the advocates of this premise believe that humankind is ethically obligated to attempt transcending its biological limitations. The most common thesis put forward is that human beings may eventually be able to transform themselves into beings with such greatly expanded abilities as to merit the label of "posthumans."

The terms "posthuman" and "transhuman" are fairly new but are used somehow interchangeably and indiscriminately. However, posthuman can be defined as the condition in which humans and intelligent technology are becoming seamlessly one, while transhuman is more about **individuals and society becoming integrated with technology**. The prospect of becoming posthuman both terrifies and gives pleasure, says N. Katherine Hayle, a postmodern literary critic. The fear is comprehensible since "post" means the concept of being human is exceeded—that we, Homo sapiens, have evolved into something new, someone else. We're fundamentally scared, then, not on how we will look but on who we are going to be. The fear lies in the lack of continuity and the excitement on the possibility of overcoming our bodily and mental weaknesses.

Transhumanism, rather than focusing on information and systems theories (cybernetics) and on the posthuman's hybridized synergy of the human and the mechanical, seeks to find new ways to improve human life expectancies and—eventually—to defy death.

Transhumanists claim that much of their focus is on the development and ethical use of biotechnology, nanotechnology, and artificial general intelligence. Influenced by original works of science fiction, their vision of an enhanced future humanity has attracted many supporters and critics from a wide range of positions.

One of the most drastic opponents, Francis Fukuyama, defines transhumanism as among the world's most dangerous ideas. He claims that transhumanism is "a strange liberation movement" whose "crusaders aim much higher than civil rights campaigners, feminists, or gay-rights advocates." This movement, he says, wants "nothing less than to liberate the human race from its biological constraints." For Fukuyama, transhumanism overrules what he defines as "Factor X," the blend of the many variables that constitutes humanness.

Assuming that we are distinct from other species and what makes us different from other species is an "X," can we progress and evolve while preserving it? Should the "X" slow down our evolution? It is too simplistic to consider the Factor X as the "soul" or the quality that only humans possess? If yes, we should all be the same, and every human expression, even the most inhuman, should be accepted.

Maybe being human is just an internal, first-person experience. Maybe it's the capacity to feel, perceive, or experience subjectively. In one word, it means being "sentient," marked by sensation and consciousness. But what about pain? Is pain a characteristic of sentience? What if we completely exclude pain? Will we preserve pleasure, or is it even possible to still identify delight and overall happiness if we do not have any meter of comparison?

Someday, we will be able to erase sufferance and bad memories. A chip or a procedure will modify our intellectual DNA. Our memories, though, make us; they define who we are. Scientists are experimenting with manipulating animals' memories—changing bad ones to good ones, restoring memories, or embedding false ones. Will altering our own memories prove us to be less human? Transhumanism is the blend of "trans" (i.e., across, beyond) and "human." Keeping the word "human" means to retain its fundamental characteristics. Therefore, we should be open-eyed about altering the hard core of our sentience.

Transhumanism pledges to enable humans to be smarter and stronger. Technologies such as NBIC (nano, bio, information, and cognitive) technologies, artificial intelligence, robotics, 3D printing, virtual and augmented reality, and digital medicine, not to mention other exponential technologies, can enable us to create a higher-quality, improved future. Should we, as well, alter our empathy? Can we aim for exponential empathy and compassion?

A new generation of transhumanists is emerging. Many are atheist, while others are spiritual or even formally religious. Their politics run the scope, from liberals to conservatives to anarchists, and their primary goal is to advocate and convince the public that embracing emerging technology and cutting-edge science is in our species' best interest. In a mostly religious world where much of society still believes in heavenly afterlives, however, some people are skeptical about whether significantly extending human lifespans is philosophically and morally correct. Transhumanists consider that the more the movement becomes known, the more private and government resources will finance companies that aim to boost human lives and defeat mortality.

Natasha Vita-More, a well-known transhumanist, affirms that one of the most effective methods to promulgate the message of human rights to elevate and extend life is bring the arts and design into the movement's discussion.

Art involved with the transhumanist movement dates back to the late 1970s, early 1980s when Vita-More wrote the "Transhumanist Art Statement" and the "Extropic Art Manifesto," as well as many other papers and presentations promoting and addressing this topic. Transhumanism, however, is now more an intellectual movement than anything else. It's markedly less aesthetic than culture-related movements, such as the cyberpunk, psychedelic, and industrial ones.

Thus, the visual aspect of transhumanist culture is not well-known by even many transhumanists today. However, some rich visual elements abound—from all corners of transhumanist thought. Transhumanist artists, for example, have recently been rising in popularity and in number. Whether it is metal-welding sculptors, futurist-oriented video game developers, or techno-musicians celebrating life extension, more transhumanist art is being created every day, some of it in new forms of media.

Non-linear storytelling—or telling a story across multiple media and preferably, although it does not always happen, with a degree of audience interaction or collaboration—is forcing the emergence of a new paradigm for culture as part of a multimodal media system. In such a system, visual events in which information, meaning, or pleasure sought by the consumer are entwined in an optical interface.

Art in the age of transhumanism claims a role for artists as transmitters of futuristic aspiration and visionary thinking. Bioartists treat their own bodies as live canvases, striving to substitute the traditional artistic medium with biological materials, bio-imaging techniques, bioreactors, and reconstructed realities. In an era of scientific and technological challenge where the traditional roles of the artist, as well as the conventional aesthetics, are questioned, its proponents advocate a future-oriented aesthetics, often reflecting transdisciplinary works in art, science, and technology.

HYPERREALITY: WILL WE BE ABLE TO DISTINGUISH REALITY FROM A SIMULATION OF REALITY?

Can we can say that virtual worlds could provide fictional settings to test transhuman scenarios? From personal and social reactions to strong body modification, to the dehumanization effects (or not) of machine integration into flesh, virtual worlds can be sandboxes for proto-posthumans. We create our own reality, becoming what we think or believe. In this framework, what is reality?

For those who are pragmatic realists, reality is what is made of matter. It includes people, animals, things, planets, and so on. For those who are more idealistic, it embraces notions such as space and time and the universe in its totality. Reality is the status of things, as they exist, rather than as they may seem or might be imagined. A general definition includes everything that has existed, exists, or will exist.

No subject is broader to analyze than reality itself. Scientists and philosophers have explored phenomena and theories to pin down what's real and what's illusory since the early ages. The fact that we do not experience reality as it is, as science is progressively confirming, but only as a representation of reality shaped in the mind is not new. As noted earlier, according to Plato, in his "allegory of the cave," one of the shrewdest efforts to explain the nature of reality, the cave represents the normal state of most human beings, with the outside representing the direct knowledge of reality. Together, the two represent the difference between people who mistake sensory and illusionary knowledge for the truth and people who really do experience the truth.

In Plato's metaphor, prisoners are chained in the cave, only able to experience shadows of people and strange objects, never questioning what's real and what's not. One captive breaks free, though, and leaves the cave. He's then able to see and experience "what is real," concluding that his past life of shadows is a lie.

Plato's allegory is still pertinent to our own experiences. Actually, it is increasingly considered relevant to the present with what today feeds our mainstream media and the Internet. In any case, misinformation, hoaxes, and lies did not start with digital technologies—they've been around a lot longer. **The Egyptians exaggerated winning battles, while the Romans used to spread forged news about opponents and their victories. Christians were often depicted as cannibals, and pagans were portrayed as immoral and cruel.**

False rumors and misreports have been used as powerful weapons for millennia, and today with social media, it is becoming increasingly hopeless to separate the substance from the bogus. Not even two years ago, the term "fake news" was used most to refer to websites that were forging official news web pages to spread non-factual elements to mislead or create propaganda. The first and most famous incident of fake news is the so-called #pizzagate, a fake story that had real worldwide consequences. In 2016, the alleged writers falsely claimed that Hillary Clinton and her campaign manager were responsible for a child pornographic ring, taking place in a pizza parlor basement in Washington D.C. The story went viral, evolved into a broader government conspiracy called "pedogate," and drove a self-investigator, Edgar Welch, to ride from North Carolina to Washington to do justice. Then "fake news" became increasingly popular when President Trump started to Tweet the term to reject what he considered false accusations.

Fake news is more comfortable to digest than facts because it initiates a process of two phenomena. The first is implicit bias, like trusting people that belong to our group and which unconsciously affect our behavior. The second is confirmation bias, like accepting news that will reinforce an opinion that is already grounded. Together, these two tendencies, boosted by the "likes" of social media, can be both manipulative and detrimental. Why? They allow the belief in a multitude of prefabricated realities.

While fake news is becoming a well-rewarded occupation, a growing community of academics, technologists, and media experts have launched a global initiative. Today, hundreds of journalists and other contributors are trying to develop a strategy to demolish the emerging fake news industry.

Unfortunately, the more media technologies we have, the easier it is to falsify reality. There are video games that spell out violence as sports sessions. TV programs and movies that endorse any possible behavior, without showing the potential consequences. The new realities architects of virtual and mixed reality. The list could go on.

Even if we indulge in these layers of reality, we are becoming more skeptical about the fact that we don't really experience reality. Rather, we "experience" data that is sent to the nerve fibers of the brain, compiled, and then packaged as images of reality. For example, one of our strong certainties is causality—the idea that the present is caused by the past and that the same present will cause what will happen in the future.

In quantum physics, though, it is possible to conceive situations in which a single event can be both a cause and an effect of another event where quantum objects, such as elementary particles, can exist in multiple states or "superposition" of states—in effect, simultaneously occupying two states. In other words, it's like the electron, a subatomic particle that spins both clockwise and counterclockwise until it is measured, an action that forces it to adopt one state or the other.

What, then, is reality?

Should we redefine reality based on the all-inclusive implications of modern science? For Aristotle—who is considered the first genuine scientist in history—reality is right here in this world. He saw the ultimate reality in physical objects, which become known through the experience of the senses and that can be known on the basis of what the senses send to the brain.

Virtual and augmented reality technology, though, are progressively able to fool our brains into believing virtual objects are in our environment. And going forward, motion tracking and sensory technology will be crucial in bridging the divide between the physical and tangible world with the digital and virtual one.

What really makes the difference is a seamless adoption of haptic technology, which simulates or recreates the sensation of touch by applying various mechanisms, such as vibrations or motions. Going further, we are even experiencing "affective haptics," an emerging area of research that focuses on creating devices and systems that can stimulate, enhance, or influence the human emotional state just with the sense of touch. That means it, therefore, can communicate the emotions felt during social interactions.

Today, we live in a society where we're bombarded with pseudo-realities or simulations manufactured by very sophisticated people using very sophisticated electronic mechanisms. These pseudo-realities flow in a context where technological capabilities of what is real and what is not are seamlessly blended together so that there is no clear distinction between where one ends and the other begins. They are simulations or, as French sociologist and cultural theorist Jean Baudrillard affirmed, "murderers of the real," and the world, as we know it now, is constructed on the representation of representations.

"Simulare" in Latin means "to make like, to imitate, to represent." In modern English, the term "simulate" is mainly used to signify to make a copy, a fake, with a somewhat negative connotation, while in science, it means testing, recreate, and has a not-so-negative imprinting.

For Baudrillard, a simulation requires that a model first be developed. Therefore, it cannot be real. On the contrary, "reality" is given by a simulacrum, "a material image, made as a representation of some deity, person, or thing," so that, even if is a copy, it depicts things that are a "mere image" rather than something that imitates the performance of the real thing on which it is.

Baudrillard made this clear in *Simulacra and Simulation* (1981), in which he explains that a simulation refers to a process in motion, while a simulacrum refers to a more static image. For Baudrillard, "simulation" is defined in four stages. The first is a faithful image or a "reflection" of a basic reality. The second is the perversion of a basic reality, or an unfaithful copy, which "masks and denatures" reality as an "evil appearance." The third is the absence of a basic reality, and therefore, it pretends, with no originals, to be an accurate copy of reality. Then in the last stage, the fourth, the simulation bears no relation to any reality whatsoever—it is its own pure simulacrum.

According to Baudrillard, "simulacra" are defined by specific historical periods and run in three defined orders. The first order is the premodern period—the naturalist, which focuses on counterfeits and false images where the artificially created image is simply the replacement of the original item or an ideal image of nature. At this stage, art camouflages and manipulates nature as the reflection of a basic reality. In this instance, signs tend to have obligatory meanings and become more important than the physical. That is, the focus is placed on the sign rather than on what it is intended to represent.

The second order of simulacra stands in the Industrial Revolution and is governed by the production of these false images, which become repetitive and mass-replicable. This is the level where the robot becomes humanoid but not real enough to be perceived as human. This could be the stage of the uncanny valley, the phenomenon where a computer-generated figure or a robot bearing a near-identical resemblance to a human being provokes strange revulsion toward things that appear nearly human, but not quite right.

The third order of simulacra is the final simulation. Baudrillard claims it as the "aim of total control." What is given in this order is the ultimate collapse between reality and the imaginary. It is no longer possible to tell the difference between what is real and what is a simulation. At this stage, it becomes impossible to produce simulations because there is nothing valid to simulate. This means that the observer can no longer perceive the reality of the initial object that is being represented—a state that Baudrillard refers to as a "hyperreality," which he defines as "the generation by models of a real without origin or reality."

Nobuyoshi Terashima defines the concept of "hyperreality" (HR) as the "technological capability to intermix virtual reality (VR) with physical reality (PR), and artificial intelligence (AI) with human intelligence (HI)."

HR is the outcome of exponentially growing technologies, such as nanotechnology, genome editing, AI, and human cloning. These technologies are progressing in laboratories and are not yet fully demonstrable, although lately have attained substantial achievements.

For example, the interaction of hyperreality and artificial intelligence will produce systems able to perform tasks that normally require human intelligence, such as current speech recognition capabilities, decision-making techniques, and automatic language translation. Such technologies are still advanced or prototypes today but that will be ordinary in tomorrow's society.

In addition, the interaction of physical reality and VR, where 2D images from one place can be rendered at another place in a 3D virtual reality ecosystem, will be a common possibility. This will create an ecology where 3D images can become part of a physically real situation so seamless that physically real things blend synchronously with virtually real things, creating an environment called HyperWorld (HW).

This all raises a lot of questions. Toward what future are we going? What kind of reality are we facing? Will it be a virtual world where detecting real or virtual, human or artificial will be difficult, if not impossible, while bridging the gap between natural and synthetic will be complete? Presently, hyperreality offers a large window into the future of technology, defining what it is and how it works with new scopes for telemedicine, education, and leisure. For example, both Umberto Eco and Jean Baudrillard refer to Disneyland as an example of hyperreality.

Exploring hyperreality means looking at the way that imitations can reproduce and improve upon reality. The expression of hyperreality is clear because items and displays appear brighter and greater in size and diversity than in normal life. When compared to this hyperextension of entertainment, reality becomes disappointing. An example of traveling through an artificial river in Disneyland allows for the simulated experience of being surrounded by wildlife and natural elements. This demonstrates the ability for technology to give the human experience more reality than nature does on a whole.

One of the most famous quotes of French theorist Paul Virilio states, "When you invent the ship, you also invent the shipwreck; when you invent the plane, you also invent the plane crash; and when you invent electricity, you invent electrocution...Every technology carries its own negativity, which is invented at the same time as technical progress." Virilio is not against progress. But he is against the propaganda of progress that makes technology grow exponentially.

A critical element of the hyperreality of television pervading the viewer's conscience is based on the deception of theatrical "real time." This mediated and often-narrated version of reality becomes the perspective of the audience. Telepresence is the ability for participation in the simulated world or environment that may be illustrating this sense of real time. Simulating participation in events and games often provides examples of how this sense of reality can be altered and engaged with.

Baudrillard, in "The Gulf War Did Not Take Place," a collection of three short essays published by the French newspaper *Libération* and *The Guardian*, a British paper, in 1991, argued that the Gulf War was not really a conflict. Rather, he considered the it an atrocity camouflaged as a conflict where the U.S. military did not directly engage in combat with the Iraqi Army. Both contenders suffered few casualties, and almost nothing was made known about Iraqi deaths. Thus, he argued, the fighting "did not really take place" from the point of view of the West. Moreover, all that spectators got to know about the war was in the form of propaganda imagery as wearable weapons, futuristic, almost cartoonish costumes, and pioneering technologies. With this representation of the conflict, it was impossible to distinguish between the experience of the true war and its stylized, selective misrepresentation through "simulacra."

Baudrillard, therefore, anticipated, by a decade or two, later arguments about the nature of "virtual reality." As Bertrand Russell stated, "broadly speaking, we are in the middle of a race between human skill as a means and human folly as an end." After all, we should absolutely be aware of what we are developing—but we should also enjoy the ride.

CONCLUSION: PROVOKING EXPONENTIAL ETHICS

This book is intended neither as a treatise on ethics nor to suggest how to define moral codes. Instead, my aim was and still is to explore the ecosystem of emerging technologies and make people reflect on the potential consequences—both positive and negative—that these innovations will have on society and on ourselves.

I wanted to pinpoint and evaluate the emergence of sophisticated technologies, to assess how far technology has progressed without updated ethical principles, and to raise a call to action for openly discussing the social repercussion these technologies could have if left only to their "makers."

Since 1956, we have been aware that we can create an ultra-intelligent agent, a genius machine, the one that will surpass human thinking. Once achieved, it will probably be the last phase of human progress. From then on, this genius entity will be able to create other, ever-better machines or innovative circumstances—and likely leaving no work for actual humans to do.

A "genius," for Immanuel Kant, is a "talent for producing something for which no determinate rule can be given, not a predisposition consisting of a skill for something that can be learned by following some rule or other." In the near future, this genius entity could emerge from a group of networked computers, from bioengineered brain-like cortical tissue, or from a combination of both, humans and machines, which is the most probable scenario. Perhaps homos sapiens is another stage of human evolution. Will the next phase of our evolutionary process be a digital one?

Although the exponential progress of fields such as computing, medicine, 3D printing, genetics, robotics, and artificial intelligence promises to drive humanity into an amazing era of abundance—creating a society where we will soon be able to meet and exceed the basic needs of every man, woman, and child on the planet—we must remain alert. We should not delegate fundamental decisions to a super system. Even if such a system is precise and infallible, we should not forget that it has been programmed and structured by human intelligence—and, therefore, it either is or could be biased from start.

In this context, we should reflect on why we're so determined to develop full autonomy for machines. We should ask whether the risks of technological autonomy will outweigh the benefits. Should we have a completely different approach, developing machines that will support and help us, without the machines having decision-making power?

Every day, new debates, new discussions, or new ethics committees take place. Ethics and AI, ethics and robotics, ethics and genetics, and much more. The point is not just to define moral codes for every emerging technology—the point is to have a broader vision. To assess how much these technologies will affect the human being. We should actually foresee a framework where we make a distinction between "human being" and "being human."

The "human being," the Homo sapiens, is clearly in the process of evolving into a new species. And we should absolutely enhance, augment, and try to encourage, in our best capacity, its evolution. But on the contrary, so should we preserve, protect, and nourish the "being human"—which is our very essence, our substance, our components.

Do we want to let go of the finest characteristics of our nature, or we do we want to enhance them? We should not allow emerging technologies to affect our humanness. For each new discovery, we should ask—is it heightening, magnifying, and strengthening our condition of Homo sapiens, or does it also alter the things that define our humanness?

Being human means empathy, compassion, respect. It means creating technologies and tools that will make our species to evolve for the better. Time, though, has almost expired. We can no longer afford to wait. Ethical boards and ethical discussions are multiplying worldwide, posing question after question on how to create beneficial intelligence, how to develop autonomy to grant prosperity, and what set of principles AI should have to align with our ethical codes. Can or should we enforce our principles on a sentient-to-be agent?

It looks like an oxymoron. We aim to create intelligent beings, ones that will be completely different from our species. Entities that will have enough autonomy to make life and death decisions. Entities that should comply with rules that are tailored for us humans and accept them even if they will become intelligently superior. What if these new agents develop their own ethical principles? Why not also teach them, in addition to distinguishing between good and evil to strike a target, respect, compassion, empathy, and all those characteristics that make us proud to be human?

We should bring these discussions on the positive and not-so-positive consequences of emerging technologies to schools, to families, and to communities. We should not forget that the new generations will be the ones using the innovative discoveries we are creating today. Simply bringing ethics to classrooms is not enough. Instead, we should—and must—enforce debates and reflections, focusing on the impact these technologies would have on our condition—on our being human.

For example, if we deal with "memory hacking," the procedures that imply erasing, modifying, or even implanting new memories into our brains, are we considering the consequences that will surely alter our individuality? How much memory can we play with, and still keep our personal identity (or the self)?

Philosophical thought experiments could help in assessing if our humanness is impaired. The British philosopher John Locke, for example, can make us reflect with the "Prince and the Cobbler" analogy. One night, a prince goes to sleep in his palace while a cobbler

goes to sleep in his home. In the morning, they discover their minds
have been switched over into the other person's body. Although
their bodies have changed, their minds are still the same. Are they
the same people? Locke implies that one's personal identity relates
only so far as one's own consciousness—which, for him, is connected
to memory. Using that logic, then, even though the prince and the
cobbler have switched bodies, if their minds are intact, they are the
same persons. Thus, if the military—which is currently researching
how to modify soldiers' memories in order to deal with symptoms
of post-traumatic stress disorder and other post-war effects—can
erase or modify soldiers' memories, do they consider the fact that,
in modifying part of the memory, they are, in effect, playing with
soldiers' individuality?

In talking about robots, the real challenge is not the machine
itself, the one that steals our work or that will try to subdue us. It is
its brain. It is the software that governs it. It is artificial intelligence.
The biggest challenge, then, is that we cannot afford mistakes. If and
when the system becomes a thinking entity—and therefore able
to recognize itself as an individual subject—it will have decision-
making power. It will be a scientist, an engineer, or a doctor better
than any other human, perhaps even more advanced than all humans
put together. It is therefore crucial that AI is equipped with human
motivations and with philanthropic values.

Let's consider Alexa, the Amazon virtual assistant, which has
managed to laugh freely without anyone having commanded it and
in early 2018 recorded a private conversation and sent it to another
user without the knowledge of its owner.

Is it a factory error, or is it perhaps something we already cannot
control? Should we be frightened? Not yet, but we certainly have
to think about it. Another reflection should be made about Sophia,
the humanoid robot from Hanson Robotics, who received her KSA
(Kindom of South Arabia) passport and who responds, winking,

almost flirting with her interlocutors. So far, her conversations are mostly predetermined, although the result is not always so certain. Perhaps we will never know if and when artificial intelligence will become sentient. Perhaps she will have her own agenda. Why should she tell us?

Genetic engineering presents another substantial ethical challenge. Even if the real potential to intervene on DNA is evident, there are no global criteria that rule the methodology, in particular the guidelines that allow human tests and that define the role of the embryo in this experimentation. Does an unborn organism have human rights, or can it be created and destroyed to allow genetic experimentation? If yes, who decides?

The *Wall Street Journal* reports that so far in China, at least 86 people have had their genes modified as treatment for HIV, leukemia, and various forms of cancer. Meanwhile, in Europe and the USA, clinical trials were slated to begin in 2018. In 2015, the Chinese also began experimenting on healthy human embryos and managed to correct genetic mutations in some of their cells. It wasn't, however, until 2017 that the United States got the green light to not only conduct laboratory research but also to do clinical applications. Why is China already ahead? Does it not have any regulations? It has them—they're just different. President Xi Jinping, following his rise to power in 2012, decided to revive Confucian ideology as the moral compass of the nation.

In the context of genetic engineering, it should be considered that, according to Confucius, one becomes a "person" only after birth and that therefore the embryo in China is considered perhaps a lesser person, therefore it's acceptable to use embryos for experimentation. Is this unethical? Should it be forbidden even though the ethical codes in China allow it? Again, on what basis should it be decided? And who should decide it? At present, it is unlikely that international standards will be established because the guidelines vary from country to country and are influenced by traditions and culture.

Despite the likelihood of them becoming a reality, international regulations are increasingly necessary. Reprogenetics, for example—the procedure that entails the use of reproductive and genetic technologies for selecting and genetically modifying embryos—can be a life-saving methodology. But it could just as easily evolve into a dangerous practice. We should perhaps reflect on the fact that we are playing with fire. The so-called new eugenics, although today based on science with beneficial purposes, continue to pursue the same objective as the old discipline—namely the development of a superior individual and the elimination of those considered inferior.

A 2009 UN report stated that out of 192 countries, 133 nations do not have precise regulation related to genetic modification technologies. If whole countries are not rising to the occasion, who, then, will monitor the outcome of this progress? Doctors? An international ethics council? Do we want to leave it to researchers who develop and use the technology of life? To those who—in a situation where blurred lines separate what is possible and what is not—will have to regulate themselves?

Maybe philosophy—and, again, the quest of being human—will not only help but also inspire more appropriate behaviour. In philosophy, problems are more important than solutions. Philosophers try to think and understand, while scientists, technologists, and innovators tend to focus mainly on their creations, without due regard to how they will influence the social fabric and the evolution of the species.

We should establish a new and dynamic public space, an agora where ethics and technology commit to undertake a symbiotic journey. An area where the outcomes of emerging technologies are analyzed and predicted, without slowing down or delaying progress. A proactive discussion to bring to schools, families, politics, and every piece of our social fabric. Once philosophers were also scientists and vice versa—science and philosophy used to learn from one another.

To find an ethical conversation that is congenial to our time and that protects us from a possible future dystopia, we should actively engage philosophers and maybe confide in Aristotle, returning to his condition of happiness—understood as the purpose of life, as the supreme good of the art of living. Aristotle calls it Eudaimonia, the elated condition that skillfully manages the relationship between body and mind, between pleasure and virtue—a state of being healthy, happy, and prosperous. Will we be able to find our core values in a context of advanced technology? Can we progress on the basis of a contemporary Eudaimonia? As Aristotle says, "Happiness is the meaning and the purpose of life, the whole aim and end of human existence."

With this book, then, I wanted to ratify that bioengineering, human enhancement, hyperreality, and artificial intelligence will be unavoidable. They are the next step for humankind. The main question is how to accompany our human evolution while taking advantage of all the successes of progress and retaining our own humanity and personal identity.

Technologists affirm that exponentially growing technologies are going to transform everything we do. We're going to clean up the environment and replace fossil fuels with renewable forms of energy—that is an exciting prospect. All of these phenomena or trends will reach tipping points very soon and will be quite transformative within the next twenty years.

We will be spending more of our time in virtual reality environments. We will ultimately be able to inhabit these full-immersion, very realistic, visual-auditory virtual reality environments, including those where tactile communication becomes very realistic.

According to our models, within ten/fifteen years, we will be adding more than a year every year to our remaining life expectancy. So as we go forward, our life expectancy will move away from us. The sands of time will run in, rather than run out.

We should strive to take this journey, conscious of the risks we are facing, and aware of the need for a new ethical framework. Technologists believe that science has reached such a level of theoretical thought that it no longer needs philosophy as a social partner. However, ethics can't proceed at the same pace of exponentially growing technologies. Therefore, philosophy should not forget its past role of the science of sciences and should instead regain its integrating role in social progress.

We should foster conversations and public debates among contemporary influential thinkers, scientists, and engineers—among all disciplines involved in technological progress. We should make a call to action, but one that also involves science fiction writers as the correspondents of the new ethical guidelines, involves artists as the propagators of the visionary thinking in an era of convergence of exponentially growing technologies.

These scientific and technological discoveries promise a better, healthier, happier future. Humankind has always manipulated its environment to improve the human condition, but these rapid changes will modify not only our bodies but also our core social structures. They will take us down the path to becoming a new species—one that we can't ensure will still be "human." And as that path unfolds, we will need all the knowledge, all the strength, and all the courage in our collective humanness to guide us towards the most ethical path forward.

He who would learn to fly one day must first learn to stand and walk and run and climb and dance; one cannot fly into flying. (Friedrich Nietzsche)

APPENDIX

When I started this journey in 2011, philosophy was a topic of my youth. When I decided to venture again into studying by enrolling in a PhD course, I had no knowledge of how much my life would change through philosophical questioning. My professors were not just educators. They also gave me a great opportunity to reflect on topics almost forgotten. Those topics, when connected with my short but intense training at Singularity University on exponential technologies, started a journey that will affect my life forever. The following subchapter is a tribute to my academic experience.

COMPUTATIONAL POSTMODERNISM: ARE WE PLAYING WITH THE BOUNDARIES BETWEEN HUMANKIND AND MACHINE, BETWEEN THE PHYSICAL AND NON-PHYSICAL?

Exponentially growing advancements may place us at the brink of a unique capstone in human history. Eventually, we will hand over our environment, infrastructure, economy, security, healthcare, food production, education, and prosperity to artificially intelligent systems.

Postmodernism incorporates a number of commonly occurring themes, including opposition to ultimate sources of meaning and truth; a focus upon surface-level phenomena due to the belief that anything more profound is a mere illusion; and playfulness in the face of knowledge systems that seek to dominate the world. It also involves language as a means for constructing social realities, placing importance upon the stories that individuals tell in an attempt to make sense of the world; the instability of meaning, placing emphasis upon the reader/observer as opposed to just the artist/author; the intertextuality, the removal of the distinction between high and popular culture; and pastiche, which celebrates rather than mocks—imitates with respect instead of forges.

Postmodernism deals with themes such as the impact of technology upon society and the effect of progression upon humanity, which make it directly relevant to the issues of cyborg ancestry and superintelligence. It provides a lens through which these concepts can be viewed. It also sheds light upon ethical issues that might arise as a result of the blurring of the line between man and machine.

German philosopher Friedrich Nietzsche is regarded as one of the predecessors to postmodernism. In *On the Genealogy of Morals*, he questioned many of the concepts that society held dear—for example, belief in transcendental unified souls and the notion that consciousness is the essence of living things. This is in line with the postmodernist focus upon rejecting ultimate sources of meaning and truth.

French philosopher Jean-François Lyotard was also concerned with rejecting revered social beliefs and ultimate truths. He went against the notion of human nature itself, using the term "inhuman" to refer to the way in which technology and science view humanity and highlighting the fact that, when people conform to a set nature, it ignores the presence of individual differences. Lyotard has expressed the view that knowledge systems for understanding humanity conveniently avoid causal thinking and instrumental rationality. He has also stated that the idea of the human world itself is artificial and that it is a product of contemporary conventional schools of thought.

According to Lyotard, it is the role of art to counteract and rectify the dehumanizing impact of technology. He believes that the functional combination of education, technology, and science are responsible for the propagation of the inhuman. He warns that technology is having a somewhat detrimental effect upon humankind, which means that the pursuit of technological advancement itself could be deemed to be morally questionable. However, he has expressed the notion that new ways of interacting with technology can be utilized in order to reduce the extent of this problem. "Simplifying to the extreme, I define postmodern as incredulity towards metanarratives," he claims, where technological progress in communication, mass media, and computer science disrupt the grand narratives of modernity.

A context where Homo sapiens and Homo Faber, who controls and manipulates nature, are absorbed by the notion of, as the philosopher Wolfgang Schirmacher defines it—homo generator, "a human being which needs no Being, no certainty, no truth." When homo generator takes the form of the media artist, it becomes the generator of human reality. Schirmacher believes that the media has a responsibility for the creation of tomorrow's artificial world.

If his theory holds true, then the way in which technology develops throughout the years to come is partially defined by the technology of today. Modern media projections of cybernetic development could predict real-life occurrences. This means that ethical thinking should be exercised not only when creating robotic innovations, but also in simulating their creation via the media—before human beings are actually capable of producing them. This empowers media as a "testing ground" for the possibilities of new realities. A concept that invests science fiction writers with the responsibility of reflecting on the positive and negative consequences of their own inventions, while writing.

Schirmacher has pointed out that homo generator can successfully "clone" human beings by putting figures forward that everybody can identify with. He has used the deaths of Princess Diana of the British royal family and Mother Theresa as examples of this. He states that these two figures were revered due to suffering: Mother Theresa was a beloved figure because she eased the suffering of others, and Princess Diana was popular because she suffered from bulimia, was involved in a failed marriage, and was hounded to death by the press. This enabled the whole of society to revel in a collective humanity and feel as if they were all the same because they identified aspects of themselves in these two fallen celebrities and felt unified by their suffering.

According to Schirmacher, talk shows also provide an opportunity for people to feel as if they are the same as others but merely grew up under different circumstances. The individuals who are featured in these shows are often extremely atypical of the human race. However, they are portrayed in a manner that makes the audience relate to them.

Schirmacher has pointed out that human beings paid a great deal of attention to the morality of cloning a sheep but are less concerned with the artificial life forms that they create via the media. Many fictional characters are very real within the eyes of their viewers. Similarly, the personas that are applied to real-life characters who are shown on television also seem extremely real to those who observe them in action.

In Schirmacher's view, media clones and simulations of humanity prevent people from facing up to authentic humanity. At the same time, they define what it is to be human within people's minds. The notion that the media creates artificial human beings that are believable to the public indicates that a form of synthetic life has already been created. It indicates that television has effectively taken on a life of its own. If it has a "life of its own," is it, in effect, a reality?

Michel Foucault is another theorist who saw numerous aspects of human societies as social constructs. His theories are similar to those of Schirmacher in that he believed that many concepts that people take for granted are actually the result of cultural and social norms.

However, although he was referred to as a postmodernist, he rejected this label, preferring to refer to his musings as a "critical history of modernity."

Foucault believed that each era comes with a set of socially defined rules that replace those of the last. He stated that these rules restricted philosophical thought, meaning that no real progress is made. Old dominant ways of thinking are merely replaced by new culturally constructed bodies of knowledge. However, he recognized that progress was being made in one area—the ability of the dominant ideologies to assert their dominance upon the populous in increasingly more effective ways.

According to Foucault, individual thought is repressed via social practices, discourses, and institutions. He believed that applying official categories and means of rationalizing things means that they can be controlled more effectively. However, Foucault also rejected the notion that power is restricted to class systems or ruling bodies, and that it is always oppressive. He held the view that it is dispersed, productive, indeterminate, and heteromorphous—comprising individuals' bodies and identities.

If it is indeed true that power is dispersed and held partly within the bodies of the populous, then it means that creating artificial bodies has the potential to alter the nature of that power. The mass production of cybernetic beings could result in power being more thinly spread. The possible emergence of superintelligent technological beings with personalities that are stored outside of a conventional body could also drastically alter the nature of societal power structures.

Foucault believed that populations within countries define the power that they possess, as opposed to the land itself. The power of these populations is then harnessed via the governance of the country. If it is the abilities, thoughts, and ideas of the citizens of a nation that dictate its power, then it stands to reason that technological innovations that either boost human capabilities or create a form of intelligence independent of human beings could potentially improve the status of their home countries within the global sphere. This has ethical implications for the development of technology. It means that inventors should be critically aware of the impact that their creations might have upon the places in which they are produced.

Importantly, boosting the power of a nation might be positive in some circumstances. However, in countries that are liable to misuse such power, it could have a detrimental impact upon the world as a whole.

Jean Baudrillard was also concerned with power. He wrote about the power of images and believed that "simulacra" can cause the extinction of the things that they seek to simulate. Baudrillard's theory of simulacrum and simulations is similar to Schirmacher's Homo generator concept. However, Baudrillard goes a step further, indicating that manmade images can help to create reality itself, as opposed to just creating clones of human beings. If Baudrillard's ponderings are to be taken earnestly, then, arguably, images are the precursor to artificial intelligence. They are as real as anything else within this world, which indicates that representations of living beings possess the same degree of consciousness as human beings.

Again, Baudrillard's core beliefs are that society had lost the ability to distinguish between artifice and nature. He held the perspective that the Industrial Revolution is partly responsible for this as it resulted in the emergence of mass production, which makes it easier to create copies of simulations and simulacra. He also put forward the notion that contemporary forms of media are not only concerned with relaying stories and information but also focused upon interpreting with people's private selves. According to Baudrillard, they determine the lens through which individuals view the world.

Baudrillard's theory is also similar to Schirmacher's views on cloning via the media. It indicates that the media is capable of defining people's personalities. It feeds them their perspectives and effectively tells them how to perceive the societies that they inhabit.

According to Baudrillard, people rarely purchase goods because they actually need them. In the postmodern era, people buy goods because of the impact of commercialized images and advertisements. This indicates that simulacra are capable of creating branding that is so powerful that it replaces necessity as a driving force for what human beings strive to attain. If current technology is capable of having such a profound influence upon people, then it begs a vital question—what effect will future technologies, such as superintelligence and cyborgs, have upon humanity?

Baudrillard has also pointed out that the existence of branded images is replacing the reality of how products are actually created within the minds of consumers. Coffee is a great example of this. Most people identify coffee with commercialized brands, such as Starbucks, as opposed to the actual plant where coffee beans originate. This is evidence of images becoming more prominent within the collective societal psyche than the objects that they actually represent. This indicates that the images are obscuring the real-life processes that are associated with their production. Baudrillard also believed that such images are covering the role of laborers in creating products.

Baudrillard was once asked, "What would you like to be said about you? In other words, who are you?" His response was, "What I am, I don't know. I am the simulacrum of myself." This emphasizes the degree to which he believed that simulacrum sews the seeds of confusion. He believed that it even prevented people from knowing the intricacies of their own individual personalities.

Although Baudrillard acknowledged the negative consequences of simulacra and simulations, he admitted that they are unavoidable. He pointed out that symbols and language build the system that human beings use to define the world. However, he also expressed the notion that they can never truly define reality. Why? Any representation of it will never be able to adequately reflect reality without distorting it. He effectively deconstructed the notion that language, pictures, and words can keep a record of what is real and what is not.

Baudrillard's belief in the prevalence of simulacra influenced the way in which he treated his own fame within the philosophical world. He never revealed in his status as he realized that his theories had been latched onto by sections of the media, which is likely to have obscured the reality behind them. Perhaps unsurprisingly, some sections of the media also criticized his perspective. Hypothesizing a bit, this is likely because media figures were unwilling to admit that they were unable to depict reality without distorting it.

Again, one of the ways in which Baudrillard believed that simulacra were used by the power was to alter the reality of war. He pointed out that war is rarely waged in Western nations. Instead, war is constantly being carried out in far-off lands. In this context, people who experience the war in images are disconnected from the facts since they view it in the way media depicts it. It makes war seem surreal to them.

The next stage after war taking place overseas and being conveyed to the public via distorted, unrepresentative imagery is war not being waged by human beings at all, as noted earlier. The next logical step after this is cybernetic warfare—which would enable humankind to experience the ultimate detachment from combat.

Politics was another field in which Baudrillard believed that simulacra were used to provide a misleading image of events. He put forward the notion that American President Ronald Reagan's popularity was based entirely upon the strength of the simulation and simulacra that were associated with him and had no basis whatsoever in reality.

"In the image of Reagan, the whole of America has become

Californian ... (though) in reality, it is not always sunny in California,"
Baudrillard said. "You often get fog with the sun or smog in Los
Angeles. And yet you retain a sun-filled memory of the place, a sunny
screen memory. That is what the Reagan mirage is like."

It is clear that Baudrillard believed that simulacra are so effective
at distorting reality that they can implant false memories within
people's minds. Even though individuals have experienced the
reality of a situation, they opt instead to believe an inaccurate
representation of it. If this is indeed the case, then simulacra are
clearly a powerful tool within the hands of governments, such as the
Reagan regime.

Baudrillard claimed that governing entails providing acceptable
symbols of credibility, as opposed to actually being credible. He
likened it to advertising. Given the fact that he believed that the
media were responsible for stripping away reality, this indicates
the way in which he believed that people within positions of power
manipulate imagery in order to retain effective control of the
masses.

"Americans are no keener than anyone else today to think
about whether they believe in the merits of their leaders, or even in
the reality of power," wrote Baudrillard. "Governing today... is like
advertising and it is the same effect that is achieved – commitment
to a scenario, whether it be a political or an advertising scenario...
leaders must produce all the signs of the advertising 'look'... Even
illness can become part of this 'look', as for example with Reagan's
cancer. By contrast, political weakness or stupidity are of no
importance. Image alone counts."

This statement indicates that Baudrillard believes that simulacra
are not just images, language, or television programs; they also
manifest themselves within what aspects of themselves public
figures choose to show. These public figures, though, can transform
their public images into something that is wholly unreflective of their

actual character.

Politicians are often said to speak with a forked tongue. However, Baudrillard's theory holds that it is not just what they say that distorts reality—it is every facet of their public appearances and the way they present themselves. He believed that the role of politicians is simply to self-promote themselves.

Baudrillard was particularly critical of the way Americans use simulacra. He believed that they think of themselves as being the masters of reality and having a monopoly on it due to their dominance of the media. Baudrillard thought that this makes the Americans defensive of their position. He held the perspective that it can sometimes make them dismissive of representations from other nations, particularly those within Europe.

Baudrillard's work hints at an age in which humankind's media creations function independently. This implies that they take on some form of sentience. It indicates that man is no longer the master of technology. Instead, technology now occupies the throne and rules over society.

Schirmacher has hypothesized that the postmodern era has reached an end and stated that philosophers must now seek to look beyond postmodernity. Lyotard was once asked what he thought would follow postmodernity. "After postmodernity comes modernity," he replied. This response was somewhat cryptic and was not taken particularly seriously at the time. Perhaps he was making a statement that all philosophical ideologies revolve in cycles. It is notable that Nietzsche toyed with the notion that everything in existence cycles round and believed that knowledge systems come and go. Therefore, it is possible to draw a logical conclusion that the ideology that came before postmodernity will come back at some point in the future.

However, Schirmacher has put forward the notion that Lyotard simply meant that a new form of modernity will come about after postmodernity. He termed this new era the "other modernity" and stated that it will be a time in which artificial life comes into being. If this is true, then it means that the postmodern era is effectively the predecessor of a period in which cyborgs and superintelligence become reality.

Schirmacher has stated that whether public acceptance and ethics criticize or openly accept the new age of artificial life is irrelevant and characterized by anthropocentrism. He believes that the technological inhabitants of the age beyond the postmodernist era will pose significant philosophical questions—as they are neither human nor a higher power of some sort, but yet represent a higher stage of evolution. The era beyond postmodernity will clearly be one in which technology plays an increasingly prominent role. Perhaps it will be the era in which humankind's creations take center stage.

Professor of philosophy Paul Crowther has also hypothesized that the era that follows postmodernism might be one in which artificial life comes into its own. He has proposed that the rejection of objectivity central to postmodernism could become redundant due to technological implants that enable human beings to store images, sounds, and thoughts in a manner that records them perfectly. This would mean that their recall of events had no elements of subjectivity involved in it.

According to Crowther, this move away from postmodern rejection of objectivity to a purely objective mind state has the potential to dehumanize people as it is their subjectivity that makes them human. This is in line with Lyotard's theories about the inhuman. Crowther fears that this new species would not tolerate their subjective human creators and would be likely to attempt to eradicate them. It indicates that the era beyond postmodernism is in danger of becoming one in which human beings are a thing of the past.

In 1969, Albert Rosenfeld coined the term "biosoprolepsis" or

BSP, building on the word "prolepsis" (flashforward) to forecast how biology advances could impact society. He stated, "By projecting our imaginations ahead into our possible choice of social future, we try to anticipate the dangers inherent in biomedical advance[s], and to forestall them by our foresight."

Rosenfeld's study sought to answer the following questions:

1. How will we protect the complex relationships people will develop with machines?
2. Will a new dimension of "humans" emerge?
3. How can we ensure that the human species does not become extinct?

Our expanded technological powers demand realistic pictures of what the future might bring in order to make wide-ranging decisions. We want to use technology, not be dominated by it. and mostly, we want to evolve into a super entity that will be improved and supreme, assuring that "it" will continue to define "its" own self-concept and distinct personality.

BIBLIOGRAPHY

Adam, Charles, and Paul Tannery. *Oeuvres de Descartes,* vol. 10, 179-86. Paris: Léopold Cerf, 1908.

Alghrani, Amel. *Legal and Ethical Ramifications of Ectogenesis* Asian Journal of WTO & International Health Law and Policy 2 (2007): 189.

AllAboutScience.com. *Darwin's Theory of Evolution: A Theory in Crisis.* http://www.darwins-theory-of-evolution.com/.

Allen, Colin. *David J. Gunkel, The Machine Question: Critical Perspectives on AI, Robots, and Ethics.* Notre Dame Philosophical Reviews 13 (2013). http://ndpr.nd.edu/news/37494-the-machine-question-critical-perspectives-on-ai-robots-and-ethics.

Allen, Paul, and Mark Greaves. *The Singularity Isn't Near.* MIT Technology Review 12 (October 2011). http://www.technologyreview.com/view/425733/paul-allen-the-singularity-isnt-near/

Andrews, Evan. *7 Early Robots and Automatons.* History Channel website. October 28, 2014. http://www.history.com/news/history-lists/7-early-robots-and-automatons.

Appel, Jacob M. *Toward an Ethical Eugenics: The Case for MandatoryPreimplantation Genetic Selection* (JONA'S healthcare law, ethics and regulation 14, no. 1, 2012) p. 7-13

Armitage, John. *Discourse Networks to Cultural Mathematics. An Interview with Friedrich A. Kittler.* Theory, Culture and Society 23, no. 7-8 (2003): 35-36. http://monoskop.org/images/7/73/Armitage_John_2006_From_Discourse_Networks_to_Cultural_Mathematics_An_Interview_with_Friedrich_A_Kittler.pdf.

Aylesworth, Gary. *Postmodernism.* In Stanford Encyclopedia of Philosophy. http://plato.stanford.edu/entries/postmodernism/.

Badagliacco, Joanna M., and Carey D. Ruiz. *Impoverished Appalachia and Kentucky Genomes: What Is at Stake? How do Feminists Reply?* New Genetics and Society 25, no. 2 (2006): 209-226.

Baillet, Adrien. *La Vie de M. Descartes* (Paris: Daniel Hortemeles, 1693): L. II, c. II, pp. 91-92

Bailey, Ronald. *Transhumanism: The Most Dangerous Idea? Why Striving to Be More Than Human Is Human.* (Reason. August 25, 2004) http://reason.com/archives/2004/08/25/transhumanism-the-most-dangero.

Ball, Philip. *The Devil's Doctor: Paracelsus and the World of Renaissance Magic and Science.* Reprint: Random House, 2014.

Ballew, Harold. *Decoding Eden.* Bloomington: WestBow Press, 2013.

David Bardell. *Some Ancient-Greek Ideas on Evolution* (American Biology Teacher 56, no. 4, 1994) p. 198.

Battuelo, Patrick. *The Infamous Rene Descartes.* The Examiner. August 7, 2010. http://www.examiner.com/article/the-infamous-rene-descartes.

Baudrillard, Jean. *America,* 108. London: Verso, 1988.

Baudrillard, Jean. *The Gulf War did Not Take Place.* In Jean Baudrillard: Selected Writings, 235, 2nd ed. Stanford: Stanford University Press, 2001.

Baudrillard, Jean. Quoted in Richard Pope, *Baudrillard's Simulacrum: Of War, Terror, and Obituaries.* International Journal of Baudrillard Studies 4, no. 3 (2007), http://www.ubishops.ca/baudrillardstudies/vol4_3/v4-3-article27b-pope.html#_edn1; quoted in Steven Poole, "Obituary: Jean Baudrillard," The Guardian, March 7, 2007. http://www.theguardian.com/news/2007/mar/08/guardianobituaries.booksobituaries

Baudrillard, Jean. *Simulacra and Simulation,* p. 118. Editions Galilee, 1981.

Baudrillard, Jean. *Simulacra and Simulations.* European Graduate School website. http://www.egs.edu/faculty/jean-baudrillard/articles/simulacra-and-simulations-i-theprecession-of-simulacra/

Baudrillard, Jean. *The Gulf War did Not Take Place.* In Jean Baudrillard: Selected Writings, 235, 2nd ed. Stanford: Stanford University Press, 2001.

Baudrillard, Jean. *The Transparency of Evil: Essays on Extreme Phenomena,* 51. Reprint: Verso, 1993.

Baudrillard Jean. "Quotes". http://www.egs.edu/faculty/jean baudrillard/quotes/

Baudrillard, Jean. *The Violence of the Image.* European Graduate School http://www.egs.edu/faculty/jean-baudrillard/articles/the-violence-of-the-image/.

Beck, Christina. *Evolution After Darwin.* MaxPlanck website. https://www.mpg.de/796674/W003_Biology-Medicine_066-071.pdf.

Belliotti, Raymond. *Jesus or Nietzsche: How Should We Live Our Lives?,* 85. New York: Editions Rodopi, 2013.

Benedictus, Leo. "Grinders: The Cult of the Man Machine." *The Guardian*, August 19, 2012. http://www.theguardian.com/technology/shortcuts/2012/ aug/19/ grinders-cult-of-man machine.

Bentham, Jeremy. *The Panopticon Writings*, 29-95. Ed. Miran Bozovic. London: Verso, 1995.

Bergman, Jerry. "Evolutionary Naturalism: An Ancient Idea" *Answers in Genesis*. https://answersingenesis.org/theory-of-evolution/ evolutionary-naturalism-an-ancient-idea/.

Best, Steven, and Douglas Kellner. *Postmodern Theory*. New York: Guildford Publications, 1991. http://pages.gseis.ucla.edu/faculty/kellner/ pomo/ch2. html.

Bierce, Ambrose. *The Devil's Dictionary, Tales, and Memoirs*. Library of America, *Library of America, Sep 1, 2011. Ebook.*

Bjorkman, Mats, and Carl-Fredrik Mandenius. *Biomechatronic Design in Biotechnology*. New York, NY: Wiley, 2011. Chap. 1, 1.2

Bosser, Tom, and David MacFarland. *Intelligent Behavior in Animals and Robots*. Cambridge: MIT Press, 1993.

Bostrom, Nick. "Nick Bostrom on Artificial Intelligence," (*OUPblog*, September 8, 2014) Ahttp://blog.oup.com/2014/09/interview-nick-bostrom-superintelligence/Bostrom.

Bostrom, Nick. "*Nick Bostrom Says We Should Trust Our Future Robot Overlords*. http://spectrum.ieee.org/podcast/robotics/artificial-intelligence/nick-bostrom-says-we-should-trust-our-future-robot-overlords

Bostrom, Nick. *Are You Living in a Computer Simulation?* Philosophical Quarterly 53, no. 211 (2003): 243-255. http://www.simulationargument.com/simulation. html.

Bostrom, Nick. *In Defence of Posthuman Dignity*. Bioethics 19, no. 3 (2007): 202-214.

Bostrom, Nick. *Infinite Ethics*. Analysis and Metaphysics 10 (2011): 9-59. http:// www.nickbostrom.com/ethics/infinite.pdf.

Bostrom, Nick. *The Future of Humanity*. NickBostrom.com, 2007. http://www. nickbostrom.com/papers/future.pdf.

Bostrom, *Nick. Transhumanism: The World's Most Dangerous Idea?* Foreign Policy (2004) http://www.nickbostrom.com/papers/dangerous.html.

Bostrom, Nick. *When Machines Outsmart Humans*. Futures 37, no. 7 (2000): 759-764. http://www.nickbostrom.com/2050/outsmart.html.

Bostrom, Nick. *Why I Want to be a Posthuman When I Grow Up?* In Medical Enhancement and Posthumanity, Springer, 2008, eds. Bert Gordijn and Ruth Chadwick, 107-137. http://www.nickbostrom.com/posthuman.pdf.

Brett, Gerard. *The Automata in the Byzantine 'Throne of Solomon.* Speculum 29, no. 3 (1954): 477-487.

Bryant, Lance, and JoAnn Ward. *Caesar Ciphers: An Introduction to Cryptography. Purdue University* website, 2006. http://www.purdue.edu/discoverypark/ gk12/downloads/Cryptography.pdf

Bugaj, Stephan Vladimir, and Ben Goertzel. *Five Ethical Imperatives and their Implications for Human-AGI Interaction.* Novamente LLC and AGI Research Institute, Washington, DC). Spectrum, December 4, 2014. http://goertzel.org/ dynapsyc/2007/Five_Ethical_Imperatives_svbedit.htm

Burdett, Carolyn. *Post Darwin: Social Darwinism, Degeneration, Eugenics.* British Library website. http://www.bl.uk/romantics-and-victorians/ articles/post-darwin-social-darwinism-degeneration-eugenics.

Burdon Sanderson Haldane, John. *Daedalus, or, Science and the Future.* https://www.marxists.org/archive/haldane/works/1920s/ daedalus.htm.

Burrows, Matthew. *We Are Playing God with a Declassified Future.* Scientific American, September 12, 2014. http://www.scientificamerican.com/article/ we-are-playing-god-with-a-declassified-future-excerpt/.

Cain, Ruth. *This growing genetic disaster: obesogenic mothers, the obesity 'epidemic' and the persistence of eugenics.* Studies in the Maternal 5, no. 2, 2013. https://kar.kent.ac.uk/43453/1/Cain_SiM_5%282%292013.pdf

Čapek, Karel. *RUR: Rossum's Universal Replicants.* 1920. http://preprints. readingroo.ms/RUR/rur.pdf

Carlson , Elof Axel. *The Unfit: A History of a Bad Idea.* New York: CSHL Press, *(2001): 20*

Carlson, Elof. *Scientific Origins of Eugenics.* State University of New York at Stony Brook, 2007. http://www.eugenicsarchive.org/html/eugenics/ essay2text. html.

Cass, Stephen. *Nick Bostrom Says We Should Trust Our Future Robot Overlords. IEEE Spectrum,* December 4, 2014. PART_2_June 22.doc. http://spectrum.ieee. org/ podcast/robotics/artificial-intelligence/nick-bostrom-says-we-should-trust-our-future-robot-overlords.

Cavaglion Gabriel. *Fu Cesare Lombroso antisemita?* Journal for the Study of Antisemitism, *(2011)* http://www.nolombroso.org/press/Traduzione_

Cavaglion_02.pdf

Cesana, Andreas. *Jaspers' Concept of Philosophical Faith: A New Synthesis?* In Philosophical Faith and the Future of Humanity, 105. Eds. Alan Olson, Gregory Walters and Helmut Wautischer. New York: Springer, 2012.

Chalmers, David. *The Singularity: A Philosophical Analysis.* Journal of Consciousness Studies 17 (2010): 7-65.

Clynes, Manfred, and Nathan Kline. *Cyborgs and Space*, 26-76. Astronautics, 1960.

Colbert, Stephen. *Morality Lessons for Robots.* Institute for Ethics and Emerging Technologies website, September 17, 2014. http://ieet.org/index.php/IEET/more/colbert20140917

Coleman, Stephen. *The Ethics of Artificial Uteruses.* Australian Journal of Professional and Applied Ethics 6, 2004): 71-81.

Cook, David. *Paul Virilio: The Politics of 'Real Time* (2003) *http://www.ctheory.net/articles.aspx?id=360*

Crockett, Amanda. *Quietly Under Control: A History of Forced Sterilization in the African American Community.* New Views on Gender, *2013) p. 70-79.* http://scholarworks.iu.edu/journals/index.php/iusbgender/article/view/13661/19885

Crowther, Paul. *Philosophy After Postmodernism* (Routledge, 2003) p. 40

Da Silva, Wanderley. *Spinoza Against Descartes's Physical Theory — a misinterpretation of Descartes's whole physiological approach to the mind-body problem (Academia.edu) http://www.academia.edu/1566217/Spinoza_Against_Descartes_s_Physical_Theory_a_misinterpretation_of_Descartes_s_whole_physiological_approach_to_the_mind-body_problem*

Da Vinci, Leonardo, quoted in Ronald Del Maestro, *Leonardo da Vinci: the search for the soul* (Journal of Neurosurgery 89) p. 874-887, quoted in Sunil Pandya, Understanding Brain, Mind and Soul: Contributions from Neurology and Neurosurgery (MSM 9, no. 1, 2011) p. 129-149

Dachel, Anna. *The Vaccine Court-The Dark Truth of Americas Vaccine Injury Compensation Program (2014)* http://www.ageofautism.com/2014/11/the-vaccine-court-wayne-rohdethe-vaccine-courtthe-dark-truth-of-americas-vaccine-injury-compensation-program.html.

Danaher , John. *The Legal Challenges of Robotics.* Institute for Ethics and Emerging Technologies website, November 6, 2014. http://ieet.org/index.php/IEET/more/danaher20141106

Danaylov, Nikola & Minsky, Marvin. *Marvin Minsky on Singularity 1 on 1: TheTuring Test is a Joke!* (YouTube video at 23':50", 12 July 2013) https://www.youtube.com/watch?v=3PdxQbOvAlI)

Danaylov, Nikola. *Visual Culture and Transhumanism.* Singularity weblog, 2011. https://www.singularityweblog.com/visual-culture-and-transhumanism/

Darwin Charles, *The expression of the emotions in man and animals.* Project Gutenberg, eBook #1227 , 1998) ch. 1

Daugman, John. *600 Million Citizens of India are now enrolled with Biometric ID.* SPIE Newsroom, University of Cambridge). http://spie.org/x108321.xml

DeAngelis, Stephen F. *Artificial Intelligence: The Past and Future p. 1.* Enterra, June 5 2012. https://www.enterrasolutions.com/blog/artificial-intelligence-the-past-and-future-part-1/

De la Fontana, Giovanni. *Bellicorum instrumentorum liber, cum figuris et fictitys litoris conscriptus.* http://daten.digitale-sammlungen.de/~db/0001/bsb00013084/images/index.html?id=00013084&fip=67.164.64.97&no=4&seite=21

Descartes, René *Biography.* http://www.egs.edu/library/renedescartes/biography/)

Descartes, René. *Description of the Human Body*, ed. Stephen Gaukroger. Cambridge University Press *pp. 170-205*

Descartes, Rene. *Principles de la Philosophie.* (§169), Quoted in Thomas Huxley. *On the Hypothesis that Animals Are Automata, and Its History.* (1874). http://alepho.clarku.edu/huxley/CE1/AnAuto.html.

Diamandis, Peter H. and Kotler Steven. *Bold: How to Go Big, Create Wealth and Impact the World.* Simon and Shuster, NY, 2015. Audiobook

Diamandis, Peter. *The World in 2025: 8 Predictions for the Next 10 Years.* SingularityHub, 11 May 2015. http://singularityhub.com/2015/05/11/the-world-in-2025-8-predictions-for-the-next-10-years/

Dick, Philip K. *How To Build A Universe That Doesn't Fall Apart Two Days Later.* Speech in Paris in 1978. http://deoxy.org/pkd_how2build.htm

Haraway, Donna. *A Cyborg Manifesto. Science, Technology, and Socialist Feminist in the Late Twentieth Century.* New York: Routlege, 1991). http://www.egs.edu/faculty/donna-haraway/articles/donna-haraway-a-cyborg-manifesto/.

Haraway, Donna. *The Haraway Reader. New York:* Routledge, 2003

Haraway, Donna. *Simians, Cyborgs, and Women.* New York: Routledge, 1991 http://

www.egs.edu/faculty/donna-haraway/articles/donna-haraway-a-cyborg-manifesto/, 149-181

Dorrier, Jason. *Artificial Intelligence Evolving From Disappointing to Disruptive.* http://singularityhub.com/2014/11/20/summit-europe-artificial-intelligence-evolving-from-disappointing-to-disruptive/

Dowden, Bradley, and James Fieser *History of Evolution.* Internet Encyclopedia of Philosophy. http://www.iep.utm.edu/evolutio/

Dvorsky, George. *9 Historical Figures Who May Have Predicted Our Future.* io9 We come from the Future, 10.1.2012. http://io9.com/5947687/nine-futurists-whose-centuries-old-predictions-were-ahead-oftheir-times

Eco, Umberto. *Travels in Hyper-Reality.* Translation W. Weaver, London: Picador, 1986. p.44

Ekman, Paul. *Darwin's contributions to our understanding of emotional expressions.* Philosophical Transaction, The Royal Society London, Biology Science, 2009. p. 3449–3451

Ekman, Paul and Wallace V. Friesen, *Constants across Cultures in the Face and Emotion. Journal of Personality and Social Psychology 1971. P. 124–39

Elden, Stuart. *Plague, panopticon, police.* Surveillance & Society 1, no. 3 2002. p. 240-253

Enriquez, Juan and Gullans, Steve. *Evolving ourselves.* New York: Portfolio Penguin, 2015. p. 268

Enriquez, Juan. *The Next Species of Human* (TED website, February 2009. http://www.ted.com/talks/juan_enriquez_shares_mindboggling_new_science?language=en#t-1023162

Ernst Mayr. *One Long Argument.* Cambridge: Harvard University Press, 1993. p. 1

Evan Andrews. *7 Early Robots and Automatons.* History Channel website, 28October, 2014. http://www.history.com/news/history-lists/7-early-robots-and-automatons

Evans, Claire. *Meat Machines: Body-Building, Cyborgs and Grinders. Uncube,* September 10, 2014. http://www.uncubemagazine.com/blog/14274527

Evans, Woody. *Information Dynamics in Virtual Worlds: Gaming and Beyond,* Google eBook p. 11

Eveleth, Rose. *Robots: Is the uncanny valley real?* BBC Future, 2013. http://www.bbc.com/future/story/20130901-is-the-uncanny-valley-real

Farabee M.J. *Development of Evolutionary Theory.* *http://www2.estrellamountain.edu/faculty/farabee/BIOBK/BioBookEVOLII.* *html*

Feigelfeld, Paul and Jussi Parikka. *Kittler on the NSA.* Theory, Culture & Society, 2014.

Felluga, Dino. *Introductory Guide to Critical Theory.* Purdue University College of *Liberal Arts website, 2011). https://www.cla.purdue.edu/english/theory/* *postmodernism/modules/baudrillardsimulation.html*

Fenton, Elizabeth. *Liberal Eugenics & Human Nature.* Hastings Center Report 36, no. 6, 2006) p. 35-42

Ferrante, Joan. *Sociology: A Global Perspective.* Cengage learning, 2011. p. 159

Ferrando, Francesca. *Posthumanism, Transhumanism, Antihumanism, Metahumanism, and New Materialisms. Differences and Relations.* Esistenz Volume 8, No 2, Fall 2013. http://www.bu.edu/paideia/existenz/volumes/ Vol.8-2Ferrando.html

Fetzer, James H. *Minds and Machines: behaviorism, dualism, and beyond.* SEHR, *volume 4, issue 2: Constructions of the Mind, July 23, 1995*

Finger, Stanley. *Minds Behind the Brain: A History of the Pioneers and Their Discoveries.* Oxford University Press, 2004. p. 79

Fisher, Ken. *We are becoming a new species, we are becoming Homo Evolutis.* ArsTechnica, 5 February 2009. http://arstechnica.com/science/2009/02/we-are-becoming-a-new-species-we-are-becoming-homo-evolutis/

Forrest, Conner. *Google and robots: The real reasons behind the shopping spree.* March 5, 2014. http://www.techrepublic.com/article/google-and-robots-the-real-reasons-behindthe-shopping-spree/

Foucault, Michael. *The Birth of Biopolitics* in: Michel Foucault, *Ethics:Subjectivity and Truth,* ed. by Paul Rabinow, New York: The New Press 1997, pp. 73-79.

Foucault, Michel. *Discipline & Punish: The Birth of the Prison.* Vintage Books, 1995. p. 135-162

Foucault, Michel. Quoted in Nasreen Niamat *Philosopher and Historian.* http:// www.academia.edu/7316133/Michele_Foucault_as_a_Philosopher_and_ Historian

Foucault, Michel. *Society Must Be Defended.* Lectures at the College de France 1975-1976. New York: Arnold I. Davidson, 2003

Frankfurt school. *The Work of Art in The Age of Mechanical Reproduction.* 2008 *https://frankfurtschool.wordpress.com/2008/02/28/summary-the work-of-art-in-the-age-of-mechanical-reproduction/*

Friedrich, Kittler. *Gramophone, Film, Typewriter.* Stanford University Press, 1999. *Preface*

Fuller, Steve. *Knowledge politics and new converging technologies: a social epistemological perspective.* University of Warwick, 2009. http://wrap. warwick.ac.uk/1306/1/WRAP_Fuller_Knowledge_politics_WP1_TEXT.pdf

Gelfand, Scott. *Ectogenesis: Artificial womb technology and the future of human reproduction.* Amsterdam – New York Rodopi 2006. p. 1-6

Gemes, Ken. *Post-modernism's use and abuse of Nietzsche.* Philosophy and Phenomenological Research 62, no. 2, 2001. p. 351-352

Gheshmi, Siavash & Shahinpoor, Mohsen. *Robotic Surgery.* CRC Press, 2015. p. 2

Glimcher, Paul. *Rene´ Descartes and the Birth of Neuroscience.* Hong Kong University of Science and Technology website, 2003 p. 1-31 http://teaching. ust.hk/~econ695/Neuroeconomics%2001.PDF

Godfrey, Luke. *Foucault's Interpretation of Modernity.* E-International Relations *Students, 26 October 2012.* http://www.e-ir.info/2012/10/26/foucaults-interpretation-of-modernity/

Sara Goering. *Eugenics.* Stanford Encyclopedia of Philosophy, 2014. http://plato. stanford.edu/entries/eugenics/

Goertzel , Ben. *Ben Goertzel on AGI as a Field.* MIRI, 18 October 2013. http:// intelligence.org/2013/10/18/ben-goertzel/

Goldstein, Mark A. *Choice Rights and Abortion: The Begetting Choice Right and State Obstacles to Choice in Light of Artificial Womb Technology.* Southern California Law Review, 1977. p. 877

Goldstrasz, Thomas, Henrik Pantle. *Computers During World War Two.* HumboldtUniversität zu Berlin website. http://waste.informatik.hu-berlin. de/Diplom/ww2/ theory.html

Goodbaudy, Trent. *The Rebirth of Mankind.* eds. Trent Goodbaudy, 2012. p. 61

Goodman, Marc. *Future Crimes.* Doubleday, 2015, audiobook

Greenfieldboyce, Nell. *Bacterial Competition In Lab Shows Evolution Never Stops.* NPR website, November 14 2013. http://www.npr.org/blogs/ health/2013/11/15/245168252/bacterial-competition-in-lab-shows-evolution-never-stops

Guarriello, Tom. *RoboPsych: Our Emotional Relationships with Robots.* Institute for Ethics & Emerging Technologies website, 6 November, 2014. http://ieet.org/index.php/IEET/more/guarriello20141106

Gurley, George. *Is this the dawn of sexbots?* VFCulture, May 2015.http://www.vanityfair.com/culture/2015/04/sexbots-realdoll-sex-toys

Hadzimichalis, Norell. *Genetic Engineering: The Past, Present, and Future', The future of human evolution.* http://futurehumanevolution.com/genetic-engineering-the-past-present-and-future

Hamacher, Adriana. *Automata: The new "sci-fi" blockbuster set to put robot ethics under a spotlight.* Robohub, 19 September 2014. http://robohub.org/automata-the-new-sci-fi-blockbuster-set-to-put-robot-ethics-under-a-spotlight/

Hammond, Edward & Aken, Jan Van. *Genetic Engineering and Biological Weapons.* EMBO Reports 4, Suppl. 1, 2003. p. S57-S60

Haraway, Donna. *A Cyborg Manifesto. Science, Technology, and Socialist-Feminist in the late twentieth century.* New York: Routlege, 1991. http://www.egs.edu/faculty/donna-haraway/articles/donna-haraway-a-cyborg-manifesto/149-181

Haraway, Donna. *Simians, Cyborgs, and Women.* New York: Routledge, 1991. http://www.egs.edu/faculty/donna-haraway/articles/donna-haraway-a-cyborg

Haraway, Donna. *The Haraway Reader.* Routledge, 2003. p. 8

Harbisson, Neal. *Cyborg Foundation.* Vimeo, 22 October 2012. https://vimeo.com/51920182

Hardjono, Thomas. Josef Pieprzyk, and Jennifer Seberry. *Fundamentals of Computer Security.* New York: Springer, 2003. p.6

Hardt, Michael and Antonio Negri. *Multitude. War and Democracy in the Age of The Empire.* The Penguin Press, New York 2004

Hawkins, Stephen. Quoted in Victor Luckerson. *5 Very Smart People Who ThinkArtificial Intelligence Could Bring the Apocalypse.* Time, 2 December 2014). http://time.com/3614349/artificial-intelligence-singularity-stephen-hawking-elon-musk/

Hayles , N. Katherine. *How We Became Posthuman: Humanistic Implications of Recent Research into Cognitive Science and Artificial Life.* The University of Chicago Press 1999.

Hayes. Lisa A. *Digital India's Impact on Privacy: Aadhaar numbers, biometrics, and more*. Center for Democracy and Technology, 2015

Hector J. Levesque. *The Winograd Schema Challenge*. 2011 *http://www.cs.toronto. edu/~hector/Papers/winograd.pdf*

Hern, Alex. *What is the Turing test? And are we all doomed now?* The Guardian, 9 June, 2014. http://www.theguardian.com/technology/2014/jun/09/what-is-the-alan-turing-test

Hershey, Alfred Day & Chase, Martha. *Independent functions of viral protein and nucleic acid in growth of bacteriophage*. Department of Genetics, Carnegie Institution of Washington, 1952. http://jgp.rupress.org/content/36/1/39.full. pdf+html

Higgins, Sonja Eubanks. *The "ART" of assisted Reproductive technologies, (in Ethical Dilemmas in Genetics and Genetic Counselling: Principles through Case Scenarios by Janice Berliner.) Oxford University Press, 2014. p. 61*

House, Arthur. *The Real Cyborgs*. The Telegraph, 20 October 2014. http://s. telegraph.co.uk/graphics/projects/the-future-is-android/

Hughes, James. *Compassionate AI and Selfless Robots*. Robot Ethics, ed. George Berkey, Keith Abney and Patrick Lin, Cambridge, MIT Press, 2011. http://ieet. org/archive/2011-hughes-selflessrobots.pdf, p. 135

Huxley, Aldous. *Brave new world*. Vintage classics, Random House, 2008. p. 39

Huxley, Thomas Henry. Quoted in Sven Walter. *Epiphenomenalism*. Internet Encyclopaedia of Phenomenology, 1987. http://www.iep.utm.edu/ epipheno/#H2

Huxley, Thomas Henry. *Collected Essays By Thomas Henry Huxley. Cambridge University Press. 2011. p. 248*

Huxley, Thomas Henry. *On the Hypothesis that Animals are Automata, and ItsHistory. The Fortnightly Review*. n.s.16:555-580. Reprinted in *Method and Results: Essays by Thomas H. Huxley*. New York: D. Appleton and Company, 1898

iCogLabs. *What is AI*. http://www.icog-labs.com/ai/#what

Iredale, Rachel, Marcus Longley, Marcus, Christian Thomas, Anita Shaw. *What choices should we be able to make about designer babies? A Citizens' Jury of young people in South Wales*. Health Expectations 9, no. 3, 2006. p. 207-217

Irvine, Chris. *The Vatican claims Darwin's theory of evolution is compatible with Christianity. The Telegraph, 11 February 2009. http://www.telegraph.co.uk/ news/religion/4588289/The-Vatican-claims-Darwins-theory-of-evolution-is-*

compatible-with-Christianity.html

Irving Wladawsky-Berger. *Soft' Artificial Intelligence Is Suddenly Everywhere*. The wall Street Journal, January 16, 2015. http://blogs.wsj.com/cio/2015/01/16/soft-artificial-intelligence-is-suddenly-everywhere/

Istvan, Zoltan. *A New Generation of Transhumanists Is Emerging*. The Huffington Post, 2014. http://www.huffingtonpost.com/zoltan-istvan/a-new-generation-of-trans_b_4921319.html

Jackson, Kibel and Raman. *Art of the Probable*. MIT OpenCourseWare, 2008. http://ocw.mit.edu/courses/literature/21l-017-the-art-of-the-probable-literature-and-probability-spring-2008/assignments/essay1_compiled.pdf

Janowitz, Morris. *Sociological Theory and Social Control*. American Journal of Sociology, The University of Chicago Press, 1975. p.82–108

Jefferson, Geoffrey. *The Mind of Mechanical Man*. British medical journal, June 25 1949. http://www.ncbi.nlm.nih.gov/pmc/articles/PMC2050428/?page=1

Jeffries, Stuart. *Friedrich Kittler and the rise of the machine*. The Guardian, 28December 2011. http://www.theguardian.com/commentisfree/2011/dec/28/friedrich-kittler-rise-of-the-machine

Johnstone, Megan-Jane. *Ethics and ectogenesis*. Australian Nursing Journal, Vol.17, 2010) p. 33

Jones, Jonathan. *How Darwin Aped Da Vinci*. The Guardian, 23 March 2009. http://www.theguardian.com/artanddesign/jonathanjonesblog/2009/mar/23/davinci-darwin-apes

Jones, Orion. *Machines Will Outsmart Humans by 2075, Say 90% of ComputerScientists. Big Think*. http://bigthink.com/ideafeed/machines-will-outsmart-humans-by-2075-say-90-of-computer-scientists

Jones, Steve. *Darwin's island: the Galapagos in the garden of England*. Hachette digital, 2010.

Jonsen, Albert R. *The Birth of Bioethics*. Department of Medical History and Ethics University of Washington School of Medicine, Oxford University Press, 1998. p. 234-264

Kageki, Norri. *An Uncanny Mind: Masahiro Mori on the Uncanny Valley and Beyond. June 2012.http://spectrum.ieee.org/automaton/robotics/humanoids/an-uncanny-mind-masahiro-mori-on-the-uncanny-valley*

Kaminsky, Alan. Michael Kurdziel, and Stanislaw Radziszowski. *An Overview ofCryptanalysis Research for the Advanced Encryption Standard*. Rochester

Institute of Technology Computer Science Department website. http://www. cs.rit.edu/~spr/PUBL/aes.pdf

Kang, Minsoo. *Sublime Dreams of Living Machines*. Harvard University Press, 2011. p. 15-19

Kant, Immanuel, quoted in Joel Pitney. *Evolutionary Influences: A Brief History of Evolutionary Spirituality.* AndrewCohen.org, 17 May 2013. http:// andrewcohen.org/blog/evolutionary-influences-brief-history-evolutionary-spirituality

Kant, Immanuel. *Critique of Aesthetic Judgment - First Part.* Transl. James Creed Meredith Oxford: Clarendon Press 1952. p. 53

Kant, Immanuel. *Kritik der Urteilskraft. (*The Critique of Judgment) Originally published in Prussia in 1790. Indianapolis, Hackett Publishing Company,Inc. 1987. p. 46

Karasek, Michal and Reiter, Russel. *Functional Morphology of the Mammalian Pineal Gland in Endocrine System* (eds. Charles Capen, Thomas Jones, and Ulrich Mohr, Berlin: Springer Berlin Heidelberg, 1996) *p. 193-204;*

Kass, Leon. *Reflections on Public Bioethics: A View from the Trenches.* Kennedy Institute of Ethics Journal 15, no. 3, 2005

Keith, Abney & Patrick, Lin. *Robot Ethics: The Ethical and Social Implications of Robotics.* Cambridge: MIT Press, 2011. http://ieet.org/archive/2011-hughes-selflessrobots.pdf, 135

Kellner, Douglas. *Jean Baudrillard.* http://plato.stanford.edu/entries/baudrillard/

Kendall, Frank Undersecretary of Defense. *Memorandum for Chairman, Defense Science Board.* Pentagon Acquisition, Technology and logistics, 2014. http:// www.acq.osd.mil/dsb/tors/TOR-2014-11-17-Summer_Study_2015_on_ Autonomy.pdf

Khatchadourian, Raffi. *We know how you feel.* The New Yorker, January 19, 2015

Kingsley, Dennis. *New Instruments of Surveillance and Social Control: Wireless Technologies which Target the Neuronal Functioning of the Brain.* Global Research, March 09, 2008

Kittler, Friedrich. *Gramophone, Film, Typewriter.* Stanford University Press, 1999

Kittler, Friedrich. *On the Implementation of Knowledge - Toward a Theory of Hardware.* 5 September, 2014. http://hydra.humanities.uci.edu/kittler/ implement.html

Konstan, David. *Epicurus.* Stanford Encyclopedia of Philosophy, 20 April 2014.

http://plato.stanford.edu/entries/epicurus/

Kotler, Steven. *Evolution's Next Stage*. Discover, 27 December 2013. http://discovermagazine.com/2013/march/13-evolution-full-tilt

Kotler, Steven. *The Feel-Good Switch: The Radical Future of Emotion.* SingularityHub, 2015. http://singularityhub.com/2015/03/23/the-feel-good-switch-the-radical-future-of-emotion/

Krafft, Amy. *Tularemia*. In W*eapons of Mass Destruction*, ed. Eric Croddy, JeffreyLarsen and James Wirtz, Santa Barbara: ABC-CLIO, 2005. p. 289

Kurzweil, Ray. *Don't Fear Artificial Intelligence*. Time, 19 December 2014. http://time.com/3641921/dont-fearartificial-intelligence/

Kurzweil, Ray. *The Law of Accelerating Returns*. 7 March 2007. http://www.kurzweilai.net/the-law-of-accelerating-returns

Ray Kurzweil. EarthnSky podcast, 2008. http://earthsky.org/humanworld/ray-kurzweils-vision-of-the-future

Kuskis, Alex. *Friedrich Kittler and the rise of the machine*. McLuhan Galaxy, 29 December 2011. https://mcluhangalaxy.wordpress.com/2011/12/29/marshall-mcluhan-friedrich-kittler-paul-virilio-2/

La Mettrie, Julien. *L'Histoire naturelle de l'âme*. 1745, p. 74-76

La Mettrie, Julien. *Man – Machine*. Cambridge University Press, 2015. p. 1-17

LaGrandeur, Kevin. *What is the Difference between Posthumanism andTranshumanism?* Institute for Ethics and Emerging Technologies, 2014. http://ieet.org/index.php/IEET/print/9332

Lamb, Robert. *10 Scariest Bioweapons*. Stuff to Blow Your Mind, April 2013. http://www.stufftoblowyourmind.com/blog/list/10-scariest-bioweapons/

Lane, Christopher. *Evolution Before Darwin*. Psychology Today, 28 March 2012. https://www.psychologytoday.com/blog/sideeffects/201203/evolution-darwin

Lang, Ian. *Boston Dynamics' Spot Ignites Robot Ethics Debate*. Feb. 16, 2015. http://www.askmen.com/news/tech/boston-dynamics-spot-ignites-robot-ethics-debate.html

Langford, Sarah. *An end to abortion? A feminist critique of the ectogenetic solution'to abortion*. Women's Studies International Forum, vol. 31, no. 4, Pergamon, 2008. p. 263-269

Lazzarato, Maurizio. *From biopower to biopolitics*. The Warwick Journal of

Philosophy 13, no. 8 2002. http://www.generation-online.org/c/fcbiopolitics. htm

Le Page, Michael. *Genetic tools you can trust.* New Scientist, 10 June 2006

Levitin, Daniel J. *The Organised Mind - thinking Straight in the Age of Information Overload.* Penguin Book, New York, 2014. *Notes Chapter 1*

Levy, David. *Love & Sex with Robots: The Evolution of Human-Robot Relationships.* HarperCollins, 2007, ebook

Lewens, Tim. *Cultural Evolution.* Stanford Encyclopedia of Philosophy, 20 February 2013. *http://plato.stanford.edu/entries/evolution-cultural/#WhaCulEvo*

Lippman, Abby. *Led (astray) by genetic maps: the cartography of the human genome and health care.* Social Science & Medicine 35, no. 12, 1992. p.1469-1476

Lokhorst, Gert-Jan. *Descartes and the Pineal Gland.* The Stanford Encyclopedia of *Philosophy.* Last updated Septmeber 18 2013. http://plato.stanford.edu/entries/pineal-gland/

Lombardo, Paul A. *Three generations, no imbeciles: New light on Buck v. Bell.* JHU Press, 985) p. 53-57

Lombrozo, Tania. Edge question: *What scientific idea is ready for retirement? The Mind Is Just The Brain.* https://edge.org/response-detail/25290

Lucea, Justo Aznar. *Designer babies A question of ethics.* Medicina e morale 59, no. 6, 2009. p. 1099-1119

Luckerson, Victor. *5 Very Smart People Who Think Artificial Intelligence Could Bring the Apocalypse. Time,* 2 December 2014. http://time.com/3614349/artificial-intelligence-singularity-stephen-hawking-elon-musk/

Lupton, Deborah. *Foucault and the medicalisation critique.* In Medical Sociology: *Major Themes in Health and Social Welfare, Graham Scambler, Taylor & Francis, 2005. p. 245-257*

MacLean, Robert. *The Expression of the Emotions in Man and Animals.* University*of Glasgow, 2009. ch. 16.*

Mahon, James E. *Causal Interactionism.* Washington and Lee University website. http://home.wlu.edu/~mahonj/Descartes.M6.Interactionism.htm

Malouin, Paul-Jacques. *Alchemy.* The Encyclopedia of Diderot & d'AlembertCollaborative Translation Project. Trans Lauren Yoder, Ann Arbor: Michigan Publishing, University of Michigan Library, 2003. http://hdl.handle.net/2027/spo.did2222.0000.057

Marinaro. Isabella Clough. *Between surveillance and exile: biopolitics and the Roma in Italy.* Bulletin of Italian politics 1, no. 2, 2009. p. 265-87

Martin, William. *Re-Programming Lyotard: From the Postmodern to thePosthuman Condition.* Parrhesia 8, 2009. p. 60-61,

McCoy, Terrence. *A Computer Just Passed The Turing Test In Landmark Trial.* The Washington Post, 9 June 2014. http://www.washingtonpost.com/news/morning-mix/wp/2014/06/09/a-computer-just-passed-the-turing-test-in-landmark-trial/

Merel, Noorman. *Computing and Moral Responsibility.* Stanford Encyclopediaof Philosophy, 18 July 2012. http://plato.stanford.edu/entries/computing-responsibility/#ChaMorRes

Merel, Noorman. *Limits to the Autonomy of Agents.* Proceedings of the Conference on Current Issues in Computing and Philosophy, 65-75. The Netherlands: Maastricht University, 2008.

Meyer, *Ilan H. Prejudice, Social Stress, and Mental Health in Lesbian, Gay, andBisexual Populations: Conceptual Issues and Research Evidence.* 2007. http://www.ncbi.nlm.nih.gov/pmc/articles/PMC2072932

Minsky, Marvin. *Immortal Minds are a Matter of Time,* YouTube, 15 February, *https://www.youtube.com/watch?v=3lTE08vb1wI*

Montandon, Adam. http://www.adammontandon.com/cyborgs-and-stem-cells/)

More, Max & Vita-More, Natasha. *The Transhumanist Reader: Classical andContemporary Essays on the Science. Technology, and Philosophy of the Human Future.* John Wiley & Sons, 2013. Introduction

More, Max. *Transvision.* Speech given at a conference at the Museo Nazionale Della Scienza e Della Techologia Leonardo da Vinci, Milan, Italy October 2010

Musl, Elon. Quoted in Victor Luckerson, *5 Very Smart People Who Think Artificial Intelligence Could Bring the Apocalypse.* http://time.com/3614349/artificial-intelligence-singularity-stephen-hawking-elon-musk/

National Center for Science Education and University of California Museum of Paleontology. *Early Concepts of Evolution: Jean Baptiste Lamarck.* (Understanding Evolution) http://evolution.berkeley.edu/evolibrary/article/history_09

Naughton, John. Google's drive into robotics should concern us all. The Guardian, Feb. 19, 2013. http://www.theguardian.com/technology/2013/dec/29/google-robotics-us-military-boston-dynamics

NC State University. *Reverse Engineering* (Ethics in Computing) https://ethics.csc. ncsu.edu/intellectual/reverse/study.php

Nerlich, Brigitte, Johnson Susan & Clarke, David D. *The First 'Designer Baby': The Role of Narratives, Cliche´s and Metaphors in the Year 2000 Media Debate.* Science as Culture 12, no. 4, 2003. p. 471-498.

Ng, Andrew. *Artificial Intelligence: Computational Postmodernism* by Jay Hack, Prezi presentation. https://prezi.com/_vtwreakhblb/artificial-intelligence-computational-postmodernism/

Noë, Alva. *The Ethics of the "Singularity".* NPR website, January 23, 2015. http:// www.npr.org/blogs/13.7/2015/01/23/379322864/the-ethics-of-the-singularity

Nordic Eugenics. *Here, of all places.* The Economist. http://www.economist.com/ node/155244, 1997)

Oikonomou, Tasos. *Philosophers clash over the future of humanity.* International New York Times, 19 August 2013. http://www.ekathimerini.com/4dcgi_w_ articles_wsite4_1_19/08/2013_514537

Online Etymology Dictionary. http://www.etymonline.com/index. php?term=eugenics

Operto, Fiorella and Gianmarco Veruggio. *Roboethics: Social and Ethical Implications of Robotics. Springer Handbook of Robotics,* ed. Oussama Khatib and Bruno Siciliano, Berlin: Springer,2008. p. 1499

Pait, T. and Wilste, L. *Herophilus of Alexandria (325-255 B. C.) The father of anatomy. Spine 23,* no. 17, 1998. p. 1904-1914

Pandya, Sunil K. *Understanding Brain, Mind and Soul: Contributions from Neurology and Neurosurgery* (MSM 9, no. 1, 2011) p. 129-149

Paracelsus, Auroleus Phillipus Theophrastus Bombastus von Honenheim *Concerning the Nature of Things* (in *The Hermetic and Alchemical Writings of Paracelsus) Vol. 1,* ed. Arthur E. Waite, New Hyde Park, NY: University Books, 1967. p. 124

Pasek, Anne. *Renaissance Robotics: Leonardo da Vinci's Lost Knight and Enlivened Materiality. Shift* 7, 2014. p. 1-24

Pearson Ansell, Keith. *The Future is Superhuman: Nietzche's Gift.* Nietzsche Circle. http://www.nietzschecircle.com/AGONIST/2011_08/The_Future_is_ Superhuman.pdf. p. 1-11

Piedrahita, Catalina. *Plurality of Peaces in Legal Action.* Zurich: Lit Verlag, 2012. p. 40

Pigliucci, Massimo. *The Evolution of Evolutionary Theory.* Philosophy Now, 2015. https://philosophynow.org/issues/71/The_Evolution_of_Evolutionary_ Theory

Plato. Meno *in W. Lamb, trans. Plato in Twelve Volumes, Volume 3.* Harvard University Press, 1967

Pollard Justin & Reid Howard, *The Rise and Fall of Alexandria.* London: Penguin Books, 2007. p. 132

Posel, Susanne. *DARPA Continues Human Experiments to Create Military Super Soldiers. Occupy Corporatism, 10 April 2013. http://www.occupycorporatism. com/darpa-continues-human-experiments-to-create-military-super-soldiers/*

Poster, Marc. *Jean Baudrillard : selected writings.* Stanford University Press,1988. *p. 5*

Powell, Russell, Allen Buchanan. Breaking Evolution's Chains: The Prospect of Deliberate Genetic Modification in Humans. Journal of Medicine and Philosophy 36.1, 2011. p. 6-27

Pray, Leslie A.. *Discovery of DNA Structure and Function: Watson and Crick.* Nature Education, 2014

Pray, Leslie A. *Embryo Screening and the Ethics of Human Genetic Engineering.* Nature Education, 2008. http://www.nature.com/scitable/topicpage/ embryo-screening-and-the-ethics-of-human-60561

Rafter, Nicole Hahn. *Partial Justice: Women, Prisons, and Social Control.* Transaction Publishers, 1990. p. 54

Rajasingham, Lalita & Tiffin, John. *The Global Virtual University.* Routledge, 2003. p. 30

Rifkin, Jeremy and Nicanor Perlas. *Algeny: A New Word--A New World.* Penguin Books, 1984. p. 244

Rifkin, Jeremy. Speech delivered at City Club of Cleveland, OH, May 1998. http:// www.americanrhetoric.com/speeches/jeremyrifkinbiotechcentury.htm

Roebuck, Kevin. *Affective Computing: High-impact Strategies - What You Need to Know: Definitions, Adoptions, Impact, Benefits, Maturity, Vendors.* Emereo Publishing, Oct 24, 2012. p. 6

Rosen, Christine. *Why Not Artificial Wombs?* The New Atlantic, OxfordUniversity Press, 2004. http://www.thenewatlantis.com/publications/why-not-artificial-wombs

Rosenfeld, Albert D. *The second genesis: the coming control of life.* Vintage *Books,1968. p. 51*

Rosenwein, Barbara H. *Problems and Methods in the History of Emotions.* 2010. p. 2

Rowlands, Mark. *Can Animals Be Moral?* Oxford University Press, October 2012. p. 39

Ryland Johnson. *Baudrillard's Butterfly Athleticism.* International Journal of Baudrillard Studies 5, no. 2, 2008. http://www.ubishops.ca/baudrillardstudies/vol-5_2/v5-2-ryland-johnson.html

Saadiyah, Al-Fayyumi. *The Book of Theodicy.* Yale University Press, 1988. p. 280

Savulescu , Julian and Nick Bostrom. *Human Enhancement.* Oxford University Press, 22 January 2009. http://www.oupcanada.com/catalog/9780199594962.html

Schaub, Ben. *Meet my android twin.* New Scientist, magazine issue 2573. 2006.

Schirmacher, Wolfgang. Biography. http://www.egs.edu/faculty/wolfgangschirmacher/biography/

Schirmacher, Wolfgang. *Cloning Humans with Media: Impermanence andImperceptible Perfection.* European Graduate School website, 2000. http://www.egs.edu/faculty/wolfgang-schirmacher/articles/cloning-humans-with-media-impermanence-and-imperceptible-perfection/

Schirmacher, Wolfgang. *Homo Generator: Media and Postmodern Technology.* European Graduate School website, 1994, http://www.egs.edu/faculty/wolfgang-schirmacher/articles/homo-generator-media-and-postmodern-technology/

Schirmacher. Wolfgang. *Homo Generator in the Postmodern Discussion. From a Conversation with Jean-François Lyotard.* Poiesis 7, 2005. p. 86-99. http://www.egs.edu/faculty/wolfgang-schirmacher/articles/homo-generator-in-the-postmodern-discussion/

Schirmacher, Wolfgang. *Just Living. Philosophy in Artificial Life. Antropos Press. http://www.egs.edu/faculty/wolfgangschirmacher/articles/after-the-last-judgment/*

Schreuder, Duco A. *Vision and Visual Perception.* Archway Publishing Dec 3, 2014. p. 419

Schonfeld, Martin and Michael Thompson. *Kant's Philosophical Development.* Stanford Encyclopedia of Philosophy November 25 2014. http://plato.stanford.edu/entries/kant-development/

Schultz, Jessica H. *Development of Ectogenesis: How Will Artificial Wombs Affect the Legal Status of a Fetus or Embryo.* Chicago-Kent Law Review, vol. 84, 2009. p. 877

Scoville, Heather. *Post-Darwinian Evolution Scientists.* http://evolution.about. com/od/scientists/tp/Post-Darwin-Evolution-Scientists.htm

Sharma, Vikas. *AADHAAR-A Unique Identification Number: Opportunities and Challenges Ahead.* Research Cell: An International Journal of Engineering Science, 2011. p. 169-176.Shepherd, Thomas. *Friends in High Places: Tracing the Family Tree of New Thought Christianity.* iUniverse, 2004. p. 52

Siavash Gheshmi and Mohsen Shahinpoor. *Robotic Surgery.* CRC Press, 2015. p. 2

Simou, Panagiota. Konstantinos Tiligadis, Alexiou, Athanasios. *Exploring artificial intelligence utilizing BioArt.* (9th artificial intelligence applications and innovations conference, 1st workshop on ethics and philosophy in artificial intelligence, eds. AIAI, International Federation information. Processing AICT 412, 2013. p. 687-692

Simulaton, simulacra, The University of Chicago. 2002. http://csmt.uchicago.edu/ glossary2004/simulationsimulacrum2.htm

Singer, Peter. *Military robots and the future of war.* https://www.ted.com/talks/ pw_singer_on_robots_of_war

Singer, Peter and Deane Wells. *The Reproduction Revolution: New Ways of Making Babies. Oxford University Press, 1984. p. 129*

Skinner, Rebecca Elizabeth. *Building the Second Mind: 1956 and the Origins of Artificial Intelligence Computing. UC Berkeley Previously Published Works, 2012. Ch. 4*

Skirry, Justin. *René Descartes (1596—1650)* Internet Encyclopedia of Psychology. http://www.iep.utm.edu/descarte/#H4

Sloan, Philip. *The Concept of Evolution to 1872.* Stanford Encyclopedia of Philosophy, *3 June 2014. http://plato.stanford.edu/entries/evolution-to-1872/*

Smajdor, Anna. *In defense of ectogenesis.* Cambridge Quarterly of Healthcare Ethics 21', 2012. p. 90-103

Smajdor, Anna. *The Moral Imperative for Ectogenesis.* Cambridge Quarterly of Healthcare Ethics, 2007. p. 336–45

Smith, Richard. *Lights, Camera, Action: Baudrillard and the Performance of Representations. International Journal of Baudrillard Studies 2, no. 1, 2005. http://www.ubishops.ca/baudrillardstudies/vol2_1/smith.htm*

Spirkin, Alexander. *Dialectical Materialism.* 1976. https://www.marxists.org/ reference/archive/spirkin/works/dialectical-materialism/

Stace, Walter Terence. *A Critical History of Greek Philosophy*. Macmillan, 2010. p. 20

Stanford Encyclopedia of Philosophy. *Free Will*. http://plato.stanford.edu/entries/freewill/

Stevenson, Angus and Vaite, Maurice. *Concise Oxford English Dictionary*. Oxford University Press, 2011. p. 89

Stewart, Robert. *Why Leonardo Da Vinci?* Journal of Evolutionary Philosophy 2006. http://www.evolutionary-philosophy.net/leonardo.html

Storrs, Lisa. *Dualism*. William and Mary University, 1998. http://jmchar.people.wm.edu/Kin493/kinsto3b.html

Strickberger, Monroe. *Evolution*. Sudbury: Jones and Bartlett Publishers, 2000. p. 7

Sullins, John P. *Applied Professional Ethics for the Reluctant Roboticist*. Sonoma State University, 2015

Sullins, John P. *Information Technology and Moral Values*. Stanford Encyclopedia of Philosophy, 12 June 2012. *http://plato.stanford.edu/entries/it-moral-values/*

Sullins, John. *When Is a Robot a Moral Agent?* International Review of Information Ethics, vol. 6. 2006

Suryadarma University. *Automaton*. Suryadarma University website. http://universitas suryadarma.nomor.net/_lain.php?_lain=17369&_en=ENGLISH

Suzuki, Shigeru. *Posthuman Visions in Postwar U.S. and Japanese Speculative Fiction*. Ann Arbor: ProQuest LLC, 2009. p. 13.

Terashima, Nobuyoshi & Tiffin, John. *HyperReality: Paradigm for the Third Millenium*. Psychology Press, 2001. p. 4

Than, Ker. *What Is Darwin's Theory of Evolution?* LiveScience, 7 December 2012. *http://www.livescience.com/474-controversy-evolution-works.html*

The Royal Society. *Robert Boyle's astonishing scientific wishlist*. https://royalsociety.org/news/2010/robert-boyle-wishlist/

Tonner, Philip. *Heidegger, Metaphysics and the Univocity of Being*. Continuum International Publishing Group, 2010. Ch. 1

Tucker, Patrick. *Four DARPA Projects That Could Be Bigger Than The Internet*. Defense One, 20 May 2014. http://www.defenseone.com/technology/2014/05/four-darpa-projects-could-be-bigger-internet/84856/

Tucker, Patrick. *The Military Wants to Teach Robots Right From Wrong*. The Atlantic, 14 May 2014. http://www.theatlantic.com/technology/archive/2014/05/the-military-wants-toteach-robots-right-from-wrong/370855/

Tucker, Patrick. *The Singularity and Human Destiny.* The Singularity is Near website, 2006. *http://www.singularity.com/KurzweilFuturist.pdf*

Tucker, Spencer. *A Chronology of Conflict.* Santa Barbara: ABC-CLIO, 2010. p. 3

Tuomi, Ilkka. *Kurzweil, Moore, and Accelerating Change.* Working paper for IPTS, Joint Research Centre, Institute for Prospective Technological Studies, *2003.*

Turing, Alan M. *Computing Machinery and Intelligence, Computing machinery and intelligence. Mind, 59, 433-460. http://loebner.net/Prizef/TuringArticle. html*

Ulam Stanislaw. *John Von Neumann 1903-1957.* Bulletin of the American Mathematical Society 64, no. 3, 1958. p.1-49

Uttal, William. *The War Between Mentalism and Behaviorism.* Mahwah, NJ: Lawrence Erlbaum Associates, 2000. p. 58

Veruggio, Gianmarco, The EURON Roboethics Roadmap. 2006. *http://www3. nd.edu/~rbarger/ethics-roadmap.pdf*

Veruggio, Gianmarco. *Interview by Gerhard Dabringer. Gianmarco Veruggio und Fiorella Operto über ethische Richtlinien in der Robotik.* Institute für Religion und Frieden, 2009

Veruggio, Gianmarco. *The Birth of Roboethics.* ICRA 2005, IEEE International Conference on Robotics and Automation, 2005, quoting J. Storrs Hall – Why Machines Need Ethics

Vinge, Vernor. *The Coming Technological Singularity: How to Survive in the Post Human Era.* VISION-21 Symposium, NASA Lewis Research Center, March 30-31, 1993. p.1

Vinge, Vernor. *What is Singularity?* MindsTalk, 31 March 1993. *http://mindstalk. net/vinge/vinge-sing.html*

Vita-More, Natasha. *Extropic Art Manifesto of Transhumanist Arts.* 1987. *http:// www.transhumanist.biz/transhumanistartsmanifesto.htm*

Vita-More, Natasha. *Transhumanist Arts statement* (written 1982, revised 2003) *http://www.transhumanist.biz/extropic.htm*

Volker Gerhardt. *Evolution: Remarks on the History of a Concept Adopted by Darwin (in The Theory of Evolution and Its Impact, ed. Aldo Fasolo, Springer, 2012. p. 203*

Waggoner, Ben. *Evolution and Paleontology in the Ancient World.* University of California Museum of Paleontology website, 9 June 1996. *http://www.ucmp. berkeley.edu/history/ancient.html*

Walker, David H. *Medical Microbiology* (4th edition) http://www.ncbi.nlm.nih.
gov/books/NBK7624/

Wallich, Paul. *Who's Who in Singularity. IEEE Spectrum*, 1 June 2008. http://
spectrum.ieee.org/computing/hardware/whos-who-in-the-singularity

Walter, Sven. *Epiphenomenalism. Internet Encyclopedia of Phenomenology. http://
www.iep.utm.edu/epipheno/#H2*

Weber, Samuel. Kant, *Singularity, and Monolithics*. EGS, Jul 16, 2011. https://www.
youtube.com/watch?v=nlFSXWZr8U4

Whisnant, Clayton. *Some Common Themes and Ideas within the Field of
Postmodern Thought*. Wofford College website, 19 November 2013. http://
webs.wofford.edu/whisnantcj/his389/Postmodernism.pdf

Winfield, Alan. *Five roboethical principles – for humans*. NewScientist, Mag.
issue 2811, 2011. http://www.newscientist.com/article/mg21028111.100-five-
roboethical-principles--for-humans.html?full=true#.VWliX1yqqko

Winters, James. *A history of evolution pt.1: Ancient Greece to Lamarck*. A Replicated
Typo, 19 July 2010. https://replicatedtypo.wordpress.com/2010/07/19/a-
history-of-evolution-pt/

Withington, P. Tucker. *The LISP machine: Noble experiment or fabulous
Failure?Symbolics, Inc. 1991*

Women's International League for Peace and Freedom *Biological Weapons*.
Reaching Critical Will website. http://www.reachingcriticalwill.org/
resources/fact-sheets/critical-issues/4579-biological-weapons

Woodward, Ashley. *Jean-Francois Lyotard*. Internet Encyclopedia of Philosophy.
http://www.iep.utm.edu/lyotard/#H6

World Robot Declaration. (signed at International Robot Fair, Fukuoka,
Japan, February 2004. http://prw.kyodonews.jp/prwfile/prdata/0370/
release/200402259634/index.html

YI, Chung Chi. *Hyperreality, the Question of Agency, and the Phenomenon of
Reality Television*. Nebula 4, no. 1, 2007. p. 31-44

Yu, Sherwin. *Machine Morality: Computing Right and Wrong*. Yale Scientific,
10 May 2012. http://www.yalescientific.org/2012/05/machine-morality-
computing-right-and-wrong/

Zimmerman, Michael. *The Singularity: A Crucial Phase in Divine Self
Actualization?* Cosmos & History 4, no. 1-2, 2008. p. 347

Žižek, Slavoj, and Glyn Daly. *Risking the Impossible*. http://www.lacan.com/zizek-
daly.htm.

Think Media Series

New Releases from Atropos Press

America and the Musical Unconscious, Sascha Pöhlmann and Julius Greve
Beyond Reflection, Anders Kolle
The Future Is An Image, John Cavelli
HARDSCAPE/ABC, Andrew Spano
Hermeneutics of New Modernism, Lisa Paul Streitfeld
The Image Is Crisis, Nancy Jones
Languages of Resistance, Maya Nitis
Nanotexts, Tony Prichard
Media, Meaning, & the Legitimation Problem from the Eradication of the Meta Narrative to the Present, Gregory O'Toole
Media Psychology, Matthew Tyler Giobbi
On Techne of Authority: Political Economy in a Digital Age, G. M. Bell
On Leaving: Poetry, Daesthetics, Timelessness, Lori Martindale
On Fidelity; Or, Will You Still Love Me Tomorrow..., Jeremy Fernando
Surfgeist: Narratives of Epic Mythology in New Media, Peggy Ann Bloomer
Tracing Etymology: Origin and Time; Monsters and Demons, Yanyun Chen
Philosophical Ontological Framework, Rossa Ó Muireartaigh
The Role of the Artist in Contemporary Art, Chad Dawkins
Becoming Cinema: Towards a Mediatized World, Mohammad Reza Sohrabi

Lightning Source UK Ltd.
Milton Keynes UK
UKHW020544260119
336225UK00011B/469/P